Footb

Terms and ᵗ ...ᵗˢ

Ken Ferris is a Reuters football correspondent who has covered the 1998 and 2002 World Cups, the 1997 World Club Cup and Euro 2004, as well as many other sporting events. He is the author of *Tragedy, Destiny, History: Manchester United in Europe* (Mainstream Publishing, 2001) and *The Double: The Inside Story of Spurs' Triumphant 1960-61 Season* (Mainstream Publishing 1995). He has written on football for *Four Four Two*, the *International Herald Tribune* and the *Financial Times*. Ken Ferris has visited every League ground in the country, and is listed in the *Guinness Book of Records* as the 'most peripatetic football supporter'. He recorded his journey in a travelogue, *Football Fanatic* (Mainstream Publishing 2000).

Football

Terms and Teams

KEN FERRIS

in association with

CARCANET

For Brooklyn, Harrison, Lyle and Matthias

Acknowledgements
I would like to express my gratitude to all the fanzine editors and staff who patiently helped to answer my detailed questions. Many of their publications and websites are mentioned in the book. A word of thanks also to my colleagues on the Reuters sports desk who read through many of the chapters or helped with information on the clubs, including Mike Collett, Mitch Phillips, Nick Mulvenney, Trevor Huggins, Dave Thompson, Keith Hollands and Bill Barclay. Finally, I would like to thank Judith Willson of Carcanet Press.

First published in Great Britain in 2005 by
FC Books in association with
Carcanet Press Limited
Alliance House
Cross Street
Manchester M2 7AQ
Copyright © Ken Ferris 2005
The right of Ken Ferris to be identified as the author of this work has been asserted by him in accordance with the Copyright, Designs and Patents Act of 1988
All rights reserved
A CIP catalogue record for this book is available from the British Library
ISBN 1 85754 777 2
The publisher acknowledges financial assistance from Arts Council England

Typeset by XL Publishing Services, Tiverton
Printed and bound in England by SRP Ltd, Exeter

Introduction

Football today is a glamorous world of billion-pound television contracts, wealthy chairmen, idolised players earning up to £100,000 a week and packed Premier League stadiums. However, it was not always like this. When the oldest team in the League was formed in 1862 as the Notts Foot Ball Club those involved could never have dreamt what the future would hold.

While the modern game is beamed live to millions of television viewers across the globe there are telling signs in the language of football that the sport originated almost 150 years ago in a completely different age when laptop computers, DVDs and video games were not in the dictionary. The nostalgia, folklore and customs of football shine through in the team names and terminology.

Hotspur FC is a classic example of a name that would never have been chosen for a club today. Yet as the second part of the name of the Premier League club Tottenham, selected because of the fiery reputation of Shakespeare's character Harry Hotspur, it recalls a time of honour and sportsmanship long since consigned to the history books. Latin mottos, club names, nicknames, ground names, stand names, club crests, fanzines and websites all add to the colourful nature of the language associated with football. Many have associations harking back to Roman times, or beyond. Rivers, hills, fords, valleys and animals all play their part in the make-up of the language of the modern game.

Most supporters, though, are totally unaware of how their team came by the name that they shout and sing about in stadiums all over the country. They are immersed in the fortunes of their team but would struggle to explain why the club crest includes a wyvern or a white horse. They are familiar with Liverpool's famous Kop but may not know the origins of the Afrikaans word. The language of football is also rich in irony and hidden meanings. The fanzines that spawned a fresh critique of the world of football have created a wealth of fascinating insights into the game and some mysteries. How many supporters know why Sheffield Wednesday had a fanzine called *War of the Monster Trucks* or what is behind Blackburn Rovers's *4,000 Holes*?

This book provides the answers, and uncovers a wealth of little-known facts about the origins of the hundreds of names associated with football clubs. It is a comprehensive guide to all ninety-two clubs in the Premier League, the Championship and Leagues 1 and 2. (In bygone days those would have been the First to the Fourth Division, but the language of football is constantly evolving.) Not every fanzine and website is covered, since the meaning of some titles is self-evident. The Internet has, unfortunately, led to the demise of many of the more colourful printed fanzines, but those publications' interesting, obscure or puzzling names, even those that have disappeared, have been included, since they reflect the folklore of their clubs.

The book was fascinating to write and research, although many disagreements remain about the origins of some of the terms and team names, especially nicknames. Readers may enjoy investigating some of the areas that remain unexplained: the bibliography provides some starting points.

Ken Ferris
2005

Bibliography

Books

Adams, Duncan, *The Essential Football Fan* (2004), Aesculus Press Ltd

Aerofilms Guide: Football Grounds (2004), 12th edition, Ian Allan Publishing

Ballard, John and Paul Suff, *The World Soccer Dictionary of Football* (1999), Boxtree

Buckley, Jonathan et al.(eds), *The Rough Guide to England*, Rough Guides

Bull, David and Alastair Campbell (eds), *Football and the Commons People* (1994), Juma

Cameron, Kenneth, *English Place Names* (1977), Batsford

Coates, Richard, *The Place Names of Hampshire* (1989), Batsford

Donovan, Michael Leo, *Yankees to Fighting Irish – What's Behind Your Favourite Team's Name* (2004), Taylor Trade Publishing

Feld, John, *Place Names of Greater London* (1921), Batsford

Ferris, Ken, *Football Fanatic* (2000), Mainstream Publishing

Four Four Two magazine, Haymarket Specialist Publications

Harrison, Henry, *The Place Names of the Liverpool District* (1898), Stock

Heatley, Michael and Chris Mason, *Football Grounds Fact Book* (2004), Ian Allan Publishing

Inglis, Simon, *Football Grounds of Britain* (1996), Collins Willow

Leith, Alex, *Over the Moon, Brian: The Language of Football* (1998) Boxtree

Mills, A.D., *A Dictionary of British Place Names* (1998), Oxford University Press

Mills, A.D., *A Dictionary of London Place Names* (2001), Oxford University Press

Minter, Rick, *Mascots – Football's Furry Friends* (2004), Tempus Publishing

Ousby, Ian, *Blue Guide England* (1995), W.W. Norton

Pickering, David, *The Cassell Soccer Companion* (1994), Cassell

Ponting, Ivan, *Tottenham Hotspur Player-by-Player* (1993), Guinness Publishing Ltd

Reaney, P.H., *The Place Names of Essex* (1935), Cambridge University Press

Rees, Nigel, *Cassell Dictionary of Word and Phrase Origins* (2004), Cassell Reference

Rollin, Glenda and Jack (eds), *Sky Sports Football Yearbook 2004–2005*, Headline

Room, Adrian (ed.), *Brewer's Dictionary of Names* (1999), Helicon

Room, Adrian (ed.), *Brewer's Dictionary of Phrase and Fable*, Millennium Edition (2004)

Seddon, Peter, *Football Talk* (2004), Robson Books

Websites

www.footballcrests.com

www.footballgroundguide.co.uk

www.ngw.nl   International Civic Heraldry website

http://en.wikipedia.org/wiki/English-Football-League-Teams Encyclopaedia website

http://www.royalnavalmuseum.org/infosheets_nicknames.htm Royal Naval Museum Information Sheet no. 32

Arsenal

The club started out as Dial Square, named after a workshop at the Royal Arsenal in south London that had a large square sundial on its gates, but it was founded as Royal Arsenal in 1886. The club's Plumstead Common ground in Woolwich, then in north-west Kent, was near the government arms foundry. On turning professional in 1891 the club joined the arms factory in changing its name to Woolwich Arsenal. It was shortened to The Arsenal in 1914, the year after the club moved to Highbury in north London. In 1927 it became simply Arsenal, a word derived from the Arabic *dar-sinaa*, which literally means 'house of art'.

Motto
Victoria Concordia Crescit. Victory Through Harmony.

Nickname: *The Gunners*
Gunners reflects the team's origins among the workers at the Royal Arsenal.

Grounds: *Arsenal Stadium, Highbury*
Highbury means 'high manor' as reflected in the gentle slopes of nearby Highbury Hill. At the time of writing, the club is spending £357 million on a new 60,000 capacity *Emirates Stadium* at Ashburton Grove, about 500 metres south-west towards Holloway Road. The stadium is named after the airline that sponsored Chelsea's shirts but paid £100 million for the Arsenal naming rights for at least fifteen years.

The *North, East* and *West Stands* are obvious. The *Clock End* (*South Stand*) is named after the clock that was installed prominently in the *Laundry End*, as it was called then, at the request of Arsenal manager Herbert Chapman in 1930. It was 12 feet in diameter and read from 0 to 45 minutes, although the FA ordered it to be changed since only the referee is allowed to dictate how much time is left in a match. When the ground was redeveloped for the start of the 1989 season the clock was replaced by a smaller replica, mounted in the centre of the grey roof-fascia above a double-tier of executive boxes.

Crest
The current crest, adopted in May 2002, shows a cannon facing east and is a reminder of the military history of the Woolwich area and the arms factory where the club was founded.

Fanzines: *The Gooner; One Nil Down, Two One Up*
The Gooner is a corruption of the club's nickname, the Gunners, used by rival fans but adopted by Arsenal supporters as a badge of honour in the same way as their north London rivals have adopted the nickname the Yids (see **Tottenham Hotspur,** Nicknames). *One Nil Down, Two One Up* is a reminder of the scoring in the 1987 League Cup final when Arsenal beat Liverpool.

Aston Villa

Aston Villa was formed by members of the Villa Cross Wesleyan Chapel cricket club in 1874. Villa Cross was a road junction in a residential area of southern Aston named after its new houses, or villas. Aston means 'eastern farmstead' or 'estate'.

Motto
Prepared.

Nickname: *The Villans*
The nickname is taken from the team name.

Ground: *Villa Park*
Villa played their early games in the old deer park in the grounds of Aston Hall, a red-brick Jacobean-style mansion built by Sir Thomas Holte in 1618 and completed in 1635. The grounds were known as the *Aston Upper Grounds* (known as Aston Park today), near Villa Cross. The house was severely damaged after an attack by Parliamentary troops in 1643 and some of the damage can still be seen today. The house remained in the Holte family until 1817 when it was leased by James Watt Jr, the son of the world famous industrial pioneer James Watt. It was bought by the Birmingham Corporation in 1864. In 1876 Villa moved to Perry Barr but in 1897 they returned to Aston and settled at the Aston Lower Grounds amusement park, opposite the Upper Grounds, where a new stadium was built on the site of a fishpond and kitchen garden belonging to Sir Thomas Holte and renamed *Villa Park*. Aston Hall is open to the public and houses some of the Birmingham Museum and Art Gallery collections.

The *Doug Ellis (Witton Lane) Stand* was named after club chairman 'Deadly' Doug Ellis in the mid-1990s, although the change brought protests from the fans who were unhappy about Villa's progress under the chairman's stewardship since their European Cup success in 1982. Ellis was born on 3 January 1924 in Chester and began life in a poor family, with a widowed mother. He originally made his money in the travel business through pioneering package-deal holidays but later branched out into property, farms, hotels and shops. Ellis was a millionaire before the age of 40 and became chairman of Villa in 1968. In 1975 he was replaced as chairman and eventually ousted from the board in 1979. Ellis returned in 1982 and, with his son, now has an £11 million stake in the club. His share sales in the club's May 1997 flotation netted him about £2.4 million after tax but Ellis and his family are worth a total of about £20 million according to the *Four Four Two* Football Rich List, where he ranks as number 74. He was awarded the OBE for services to football in the 2005 New Year's Honours List.

The *Trinity Road Stand* is named after the nearby road and the *Holte End Stand* after Sir Thomas Holte (see **Ground**, above), leaving the *North Stand*.

Crest
The famous rampant lion and *Prepared* motto first featured on the old shield design, seen by many on the grand mosaics of the now demolished Trinity Road Stand, and are believed to have been introduced by the founder of the Football League and former Villa vice-president William McGregor. It is thought he suggested the lion, similar to that on the Scottish FA crest, at the turn of the twentieth century, to remind him of his Scottish roots in his newly adopted home of Birmingham.

Fanzines: *Heroes and Villains*, *The Holy Trinity*
Heroes and Villains (www.heroesandvillains.net) is a play on the team name and nickname. *The Holy Trinity* is a reference to Villa Park, the shrine worshipped by the fans which is situated on Trinity Road.

Websites: *Class of 82* (www.astonvilla1982.co.uk), *Holtenders* (http://astonvilla.rivals.net)
Class of 82 is a tribute to the Aston Villa side of 1982. Twelve months after winning the First Division title, using just fourteen players, they lifted the European Cup under captain Dennis Mortimer after a 1–0 win over Bayern Munich in Rotterdam with a goal from their England centre forward Peter Withe. *Holtenders* refers to the fans who occupy the Holte End of the ground (see **Ground**, above).

Barnet

A team called Barnet FC was founded in 1888 but forced to disband in 1901 after a Football Association inquiry. Their name and ground was adopted by rival team, Barnet Avenue, in 1903. Alston Works, a dental company's team, changed its name to Barnet Alston in 1906 and a year later moved to Underhill. Avenue and Alston merged as Barnet and Alston FC in 1912, becoming Barnet FC in 1919.

The Hertfordshire town north-west of London takes its name from Old English *baernet*, 'land cleared by burning'. As Barnet is one of the highest points in that part of the country, it was used in past times as a place where a fire could be lit to spread news quickly, which explains the use of a name that means 'conflagration' in Saxon.

Nickname: *The Bees*
The nickname is a reference to the team's amber and black shirts.

Ground: *Underhill Stadium*
Barnet played their first match on the sloping pitch at *Underhill Stadium*, originally on the site of Underhill Farm, as Barnet Alston in September 1907. The ground takes its name from the Underhill area at the bottom of Barnet Hill.

The stands are known as the *Main Stand, South Terrace* and *East Terrace*

Crest
The club badge is partly based on the town's coat of arms. The roses with the crossed swords at the top of the shield recall the Battle of Barnet. This took place during the fifteenth-century Wars of the Roses between Yorkist troops under Edward IV and Lancastrians led by Richard Neville, known as 'Warwick The Kingmaker', as they struggled for the crown of England. The battle on 14 April 1471 marked the end for Neville, the most powerful baron of the time, and was just the first act in Edward's desperate attempt to wrest back the throne. It is the most famous event in Barnet's history and is therefore suitably represented on the badge.

Barnet hill is also shown on the club crest, with corner flags in the team's amber and black colours on either side, with a ball on top.

The badge was introduced in February 1957 when Barnet played Clapton in the second round of the London Cup, and was first seen on the club's programmes in the 1970s. It is thought to have been designed by the club chairman Syd Price. The original town crest showed a burning hill in reference to the derivation of the place-name (see above).

Fanzine: *Two Together*
The fanzine is named in reference to the club's late owner Stan Flashman who made his name as a ticket tout and could always get you 'two together' for any event, from the FA Cup final to the Queen's Garden Party.

Website: *Bees Mad* (www.barnet-mad.co.uk)
Bees Mad is a reference to the club nickname The Bees (see **Nickname**, above).

Barnsley

The club was founded in 1887 as Barnsley St Peter's church team by the Reverend Tiverton Preedy. They dropped St Peter's from their name the year before joining the Football League in 1898.

The Yorkshire town's name means 'Beorn's woodland clearing'. Nobody knows who Beorn was but his name was probably a shortened version of something like Beornwulf, from the Old English words *beorn* (man) and *wulf* (wolf).

Nicknames: *The Tykes, Reds, Colliers*
The Tykes comes from the word 'Tyke', which is ancient dialect for a native of Yorkshire. It was originally used to describe comical rustic characters or as an insult from Old Norse, meaning a dog or cur, but it now refers to the town's hard-working labourers as well as small children and mongrels. *Reds* is taken from the team's colours. Barnsley is the centre of the South Yorkshire coalfield and *Colliers* refers to the miners who worked in the once thriving coal mining industry, including Barnsley Main Colliery which was near the club's Oakwell Ground.

Ground: *Oakwell*
Barnsley played their first matches on a pitch behind the *Brewery Stand* (the current *East Stand*) of the Oakwell Ground, where they moved in 1888. The ground's name comes from the oak trees that once grew on the site.

The stands are named the *New East, West, North* (*Spion Kop*; see **Liverpool**, Ground) and *Pontefract Road* (*South*) *Stand*, known as the *Ponty End*.

Crest
Arthur Braithwaite, a local dog breeder and friend of the players and officials, had a favourite bulldog called Toby. After seeing a photograph of Toby with Arthur and the players, Barnsley officials decided to change their crest to a cartoon of the bulldog they called Toby Tyke, after the club's nickname. The popular figure, who represents the history of Barnsley and the bulldog spirit of the English, was first

seen in the match programme on 19 August 1967 for a game against
Doncaster Rovers.

Websites: *Total Tykes* (**http://barnsley.rivals.net**), *Tykes Mad*
(**www.barnsley-mad.co.uk**)
Total Tykes and *Tykes Mad* are both references to the club's nickname (see **Nicknames**, above).

Birmingham City

The club was founded in 1875 as Small Heath Alliance by mainly cricketing members of Trinity Church, Bordesley. The name 'Birmingham' was used for the 1905–6 season, when the club moved to St Andrew's, and 'City' was added in 1945.

'Birmingham' means 'the settlement of Beorma's people'. Nobody knows who Beorma was but his name is a shortened version of the Old English name Beornmund or 'man-guardian'.

Nickname: *Blues*
The nickname is a reference to the team's strip.

Ground: *St Andrew's*
Birmingham first played at *St Andrew's* in 1906. The ground was named after an old church that used to stand about 500 yards away on St Andrew's Road. The nearby Victorian school was also named after the church, which took its own name from Scotland's patron saint.

The *Kop Stand* gained its name because when the club moved to St Andrew's they had to raise the terracing on the Coventry Road side. To do this, 100,000 loads of rubbish, rising to 47 feet, were dumped by anyone willing to pay. 'Almost as soon as fans saw this huge bank rising up they nicknamed it the 'Spion Kop' [see **Liverpool**, Ground], which suggests that either news of the naming of Liverpool's Kop in the autumn of 1906 had spread rapidly, or the name was already well known from Woolwich Arsenal's original Kop at Plumstead', writes Simon Inglis in his *Football Grounds of Britain* (HarperCollins, 1987). Birmingham's Kop was uniquely situated along the side of the pitch instead of at one end. A new Kop Stand was built in 1994.

Railway End, or *City Stand* is named after the railway cutting that runs behind it near St Andrew's school. The *Tilton Road End* is named after the nearby road.

Crest
The badge shows the world superimposed on a football, with 'Birmingham City Football Club' and '1875', the year the club was founded, wrapped around it.

The crest, devised by Mike Wood, a Birmingham fan, was the winning entry in a competition for a new badge design in the local *Sports Argus* newspaper in 1972. He said, 'I was thinking along the lines of football being a game that is played all over the world and that football is the world's most popular sport. From then on it just seemed an obvious link to me, the globe and the football. It was then just a case of adding a scroll for the club name and details.' Birmingham's commercial manager Geoff Greaves said at the time, 'It is forward looking and introduces the globe and the idea of European football, which is what everyone wants to see at St Andrew's.' Wood's design replaced the city's coat of arms as the club emblem.

Wood remains proud of his design: 'the badge can be seen all over the place and fans even have it as pendants around their necks and so yes, I am still proud of it. I occasionally do say to people that I designed the badge and they often look at me as if I am a bit mad, as I am now a plumber by trade but they then normally are quite interested to talk about it. Plus Blues are the team I have supported all my life, so I feel proud in that respect to have designed the club's badge.'

Fanzines: *Made in Brum, Wake Up Blue, The Penguin, Zulu*
Made in Brum refers to the fact that the club and most of the fans, if not the players, were born and bred in the city and the surrounding area, with Brum being local dialect for Birmingham, hence Brummies. *Wake Up Blue* is what City fans do every day – and it does not mean they wake up feeling sad! *The Penguin* was named after the old home kit of the 1970s: a blue shirt with a thick white stripe down the centre resembling the markings of a penguin. *Zulu* was named after the notorious hooligans called the Zulu Warriors who follow the team.

Websites: *Keep Right On* (www.keeprighton.co.uk),
Tired and Weary (www.tiredandweary.com), *Singing the Blues* (www.singingtheblues.co.uk), *Planet Blues* (www.planetblues.co.uk)
The first two names come from the City song 'The End of the Road', which refers to the many years of suffering Blues fans have gone through. *Keep Right On* is the songtitle and *Tired and Weary* is a line in the song:

As you go through life,
It's a long long road, there will be joys and sorrow, too
As we journey on, we will sing this song,
For the boys in royal blue,...
Keep right on to the end of the road...
Though you're tired and weary, still journey on...

Singing the Blues comes from another supporters' song, based on an original written by Melvin Endsley and sung by Guy Mitchell: 'Never felt more like singing the Blues, / I never thought I'd ever lose...'. Or, in another version, 'You got me singing the Blues / The City win, the Villa lose'. *Planet Blues* refers to the team's colours and nickname (see **Nickname**, above).

Blackburn Rovers

The club was called Rovers (wanderers), because it did not have a ground when it was formed by public school old boys in 1875 as Blackburn Grammar School Football Club. Rovers spent much of their first season without a home and it was only in mid-1876 that they settled at Oozehead, complete with a drainage pool, or 'cow-pit', that had to be covered with turf laid on planks. They later moved to Pleasington Cricket Ground, Alexandra Meadows, Ewood Bridge, on the site of Ewood Park, and Leamington Street. They settled permanently at Ewood Park in 1890 (see **Ground**, below). The Lancashire town's name means 'dark-coloured stream', from the Old English *blaec* and *burna*. 'Ewood' is derived from the Old English *ea-wudu*, 'a wood on the river', in this case the River Darwen.

Motto
Arte et Labore. Through Skill and Hard Work.

Nickname: *Rovers*
Rovers is taken from the club name.

Ground: *Ewood Park*
The general area in which the ground is situated is known as Ewood.

The *Jack Walker (Nuttall Street) Stand* is named after the club's late benefactor, Jack Walker. He was born on 19 May 1929 in Little Harwood near Blackburn. After leaving school at 14 Walker worked for his father as a sheet metal worker and a conscript craftsman in the Royal Electrical and Mechanical Engineers. He completed his National Service and took over the family business in 1951 with his brother Fred after their father died. Together, they transformed the business, which grew into one of the biggest steel stockholding concerns in the world; by the late 1980s the company employed more than 3,000 people in 60 locations.

Walker first got involved with the Ewood Park club when the then chairman Bill Fox persuaded his old school friend and Rovers fan, by now the owner of Britain's largest steel stockholding company, to help build a new *Riverside Stand*, which was opened in 1988 (see **Walker Steel Stand**, below). Two years later Walker

Steel was bought by British Steel for £330 million, the highest amount ever paid for a British-owned family business. Walker, with a personal fortune ranked among the top thirty in Britain, retired to St Helier, Jersey, but was looking for a new investment. In January 1991 he bought 62 per cent of Rovers, and became vice-president.

Walker spent £13 million in the first eighteen months, rebuilding the team by buying players like Alan Shearer from Southampton, for a British record transfer fee of £3.5 million, Chris Sutton from Norwich City, for another British record fee of £5 million, and goalkeeper Tim Flowers. In April 1992 Walker committed himself to increasing the club's share capital to £25 million, of which he would become the holder of all but a small percentage. Two months later his new-look team reached the Premier League via the playoffs under new manager Kenny Dalglish, who had come out of retirement to manage Blackburn in 1991. With the help of Walker's millions Blackburn were Premier League runners-up in 1994 and won the League title the following year for the first time since 1914.

Walker also provided a solid foundation for the club by developing Ewood Park into a 31,367 capacity all-seater stadium at a cost of £25 million and building a new youth academy and training facilities at Brockhall. He died aged 71 on 18 August 2000 after a long battle with cancer.

The *Walker Steel (Riverside) Stand* is named after Jack Walker's former company, but traditionally known as the *Riverside Stand* because it backs onto the River Darwen, hence the term *Riversiders*. The *Darwen End* is named after the small town four miles from Blackburn. The *Blackburn End* is the nearest to the town centre.

Crest
The badge shows a Lancashire rose inside a circle, with Blackburn Rovers FC and 1875, the year in which the club was founded, surrounding it, with the motto *Arte et Labore* at the bottom.

Fanzines: *4,000 holes, Colin's Cheeky Bits*
4,000 holes is named after the line '4,000 holes in Blackburn Lancashire' from the Beatles song *A Day in the Life*, which referred to the large number of coal mines in the area. *Colin's Cheeky Bits* refers to the club's former Scotland defender, Colin Hendry, who once had to change his shorts in front of the Blackburn End, sparking a tradition of the fans singing 'Colin, Colin show us your arse' before most games. Hendry sometimes obliged, occasionally during a game.

The fanzine was originally known as *Loadsamoney* but the name changed when the money dried up (see **Jack Walker Stand**, above).

Website: *Rambling Riversider* **(http://ramblingriversider. mysite.wanadoo-members.co.uk)**
The website is named after the fans who sit in the Riverside Stand that backs onto the River Darwen, hence the term Riversiders (see **Ground**, above).

Blackpool

The old boys of St John's School established a club in 1887 named after the Lancashire town, which takes its own name from a black pool of peaty water that used to lie about half a mile from the sea. By the end of the eighteenth century the surrounding area had been turned into meadowland and the stream that flowed from the pool became the town's main sewer.

Motto
Progress.

Nicknames: *The Seasiders, The Tangerines*
The Seasiders comes from the club's location near the Irish Sea. Blackpool, the leading resort in the north-west and one of the most popular in the country, is 'famous for fresh air and fun'. It is the archetypal British resort with a Golden Mile of piers, fortune tellers and bingo halls. *The Tangerines* is a reference to the colour of the team strip.

Ground: *Bloomfield Road*
Blackpool had several homes before settling at *Bloomfield Road*, formerly known as Gamble's Field after the farmer who owned the land. The ground originally belonged to Blackpool's local rivals South Shore until the Seasiders arrived in 1899 and the teams merged and renamed it Bloomfield Road. The name comes from a large house, or villa, called Bloom Field because the grounds were occupied by greenhouses. The house, which used to stand next to the Bloomfield Road pub, was a coach station for many years and is now the site of a large retail store.

The stands are known as *West, East* (nicknamed the *Scratching Shed), South* and the *New Mortensen North Stand (Spion Kop;* see **Liverpool**, Ground). The latter is named after the team's England striker Stan Mortensen, nicknamed the Blackpool Bombshell, who was in his heyday during the 1940s and 50s. He scored 197 goals in 320 League games for Blackpool and 24 goals in 25 games for England. Also known as the Electric Eel or Electric Heels, Mortensen made his international debut in unusual circumstances when he played against his own country in a friendly in September 1943, after being invited to turn out at the last minute for Wales after their left-half was injured. He scored four goals for England on his proper debut against Portugal in May 1947 and in November struck a hat-trick versus Sweden. His final game for England was the infamous 6–3 defeat by Hungary. Mortensen scored in every round of the FA Cup in 1948, including the final which Blackpool lost 4–2 to Manchester United. He was the First Division (Premier League today) top scorer in 1950–51 with thirty goals. However, Mortensen was often overshadowed by team mate Stanley Matthews (see **Stoke City**, Ground), whose name will be forever associated with his tricky wing play in the 1953 FA Cup final against Bolton Wanderers even though Mortensen was just as sensational and scored a hat-trick in the 4–3 victory. Mortensen, who served as an RAF bomber pilot during the Second World War, was included in the Football League Centenary 100 players.

Crest
The badge is the town's coat of arms, which came into being in 1899. It has been used on and off by Blackpool since the team's shirt colour was changed to tangerine. The waves and a seagull represent the seaside nature of the town.

Fanzine: *Another View from the Tower* (www.avftt.com)
Another View from the Tower, known as *AVFTT*, refers to the famous Blackpool Tower, 'the skyline's only touch of grace' according to *The Rough Guide*. It was built in 1894 complete with Edwardian ballroom, a small aquarium and a Moorish-inspired indoor circus between the tower's legs. The Tower World theme park offers a ride up the 500-foot imitation of the Parisian landmark.

Website: *Seasiders* (www.blackpool-mad.co.uk)
The website is a reference to the team's nickname.

Bolton Wanderers

Boys at Christ Church Sunday School established a football club named after the school in 1874, with the vicar as president. They used the church's name, since it owned the ground, but when the vicar made too many rules about using the premises the club broke away and became Bolton Wanderers in 1877.

The Lancashire town near Manchester has a name meaning a 'village with buildings', derived from the Old English words *bothl*, building, and *tun*, settlement. It is the main residential part of a settlement, as distinct from outlying farms. 'Wanderers' referred to the fact that the club had no ground when it first split from the church.

Nickname: *The Trotters*

There are various theories about the origin of the nickname the *Trotters*. One suggestion is that the team was once full of pranksters and therefore given the Old English name *trotter*, which meant 'practical joker'. Another links the nickname to the team name Wanderers, since the players had to move or 'trot' about from their headquarters to various grounds before they settled permanently at Burnden Park in 1895.

Ground: *The Reebok Stadium*

The club moved to the stadium from *Burnden Park* in 1997. It is named after the club's sponsors, the Reebok sportswear company, which began in Bolton and is based in Lostock, some five miles from the team's old ground. The first sod at Lostock was ceremonially dug by the Mayor of Bolton and the club's president Nat Lofthouse in December 1995.

The stands are called *North* , *South*, *West* and *Nat Lofthouse (East) Stand*. The latter is named after the England centre-forward who played for Bolton in the 1950s. Born in the town on 27 August 1925, he joined Wanderers as an amateur in September 1939 and made his debut later that year. Lofthouse developed a reputation as a courageous striker while still working as a miner. He got up at 4 a.m. and worked an eight-hour shift down the pit before playing for Bolton in the afternoon.

Lofthouse made his England debut in November 1950, scoring

twice against Yugoslavia. After getting another two goals against Austria on 25 May 1952 he became known as the 'Lion of Vienna', mainly because he was unconscious when his second effort crossed the line. Lofthouse won the Footballer of the Year award in 1953; he had scored in every round of the FA Cup, including the final which Bolton lost 4–3 to Blackpool after leading 3–1. Stanley Matthews inspired his Blackpool team to victory with a mesmerising display on the wing, and the match has always been known as the 'Matthews Final'.

Lofthouse was top scorer in the First Division in 1956 and two years later scored both goals as he captained Bolton to a 2–0 FA Cup final victory over a Manchester United side decimated by the Munich air crash. Lofthouse scored the last of his thirty goals in thirty-three internationals in 1958. He retired in 1960 due to injury having scored 285 goals in 485 matches. In 1968 he took over as manager of Bolton but resigned in 1971, before briefly returning to the post in 1985. He became club president the following year.

Crest
The badge is a very modern Bolton Wanderers FC design.

Fanzines: *Tripe and Trotters*, *White Love*
Tripe and Trotters is an ironic title based on how outsiders see the Lancashire town and its traditional foods. (*Trotters* is also the team's nickname (see **Nickname**, above). *White Love* is a reference to how the supporters feel about their team, who play in an all-white strip.

Websites: *The Wanderer* (www.thewanderer.co.uk), *World Wide Wanderers* (www.boltonwanderers.rivals.net), *Unofficial trotters – Bolton Wanderers MAD* (www.bolton-wanderers-mad.co.uk)
The Wanderer and *World Wide Wanderers* are references to the second part of the team name. *Unofficial trotters – Bolton Wanderers MAD* is a reference to the team's nickname (see **Nickname**, above).

Boston United

Boston Football Club was started in 1870 before Boston Town was established in the 1880s. The club dropped 'Town' from its name after the First World War and re-formed as Boston United in 1934.

The Lincolnshire port of Boston has a name that is popularly interpreted as 'St Botolph's stone' after a local saint who preached at the 'stone' marking a boundary or meeting place. Boston's main church, the 'Boston Stump', so called because it does not have a spire, is dedicated to the saint, although historical evidence is lacking to establish his exact identity. The church's 272-foot perpendicular tower, which looks truncated from a distance, still towers over the market town and fenland. St Botolph's is one of the largest parish churches in England.

Nickname: *The Pilgrims*
In the early seventeenth century Boston became a centre for Nonconformists (Protestants dissenting from the Anglican church after its reformation under Queen Elizabeth I) and provided a stream of emigrants (Pilgrims) for the colonies of New England, hence the club's nickname.

In 1607 some of the original Pilgrim Fathers were caught by the authorities in Boston, Lincolnshire after a failed attempt to escape religious persecution by slipping across to Holland. They were locked up for thirty days in the Guildhall on South Street near St Botolph's, which now contains a small museum with several old cells. The Pilgrim Fathers eventually sailed from Plymouth in the Mayflower on 16 September 1620 to found the first colony in New England in New Plymouth, Massachusetts (see **Plymouth, Nickname**).

The state capital of Massachusetts takes its name from the English port of Boston, which was the home of many of its original Puritan settlers who founded the American city in 1630.

Ground: *York Street*
Boston Town first played at *York Street* in the 1880s; the ground is named after the street.

The *Finn Forest Stand* is named after the sponsors, a timber company who have a plant in the town and used to also sponsor the team shirts. The *Spayne Road Stand* is named after the road behind the ground. The *Town End Terrace* is the nearest to the town. The *York Street Stand*, like the stadium, is named after the street.

Crest
The badge shows *The Mayflower*, the ship in which the pilgrims sailed to New England (see **Nickname**, above).

Fanzines: *Town End Tales, From Behind Your Fences*
Town End Tales is named after the Town End Terrace. *From Behind Your Fences* is a reference to the huge 8–foot iron fences at the Town End.

Bournemouth

The club was founded in 1890 as Boscombe St John's and nine years later was refounded as Boscombe FC. Boscombe, a suburb of Bournemouth, means 'valley overgrown with spiky plants' from Old English *bors* and *cumb*. The team's name was changed to Bournemouth and Boscombe Athletic FC in 1923 to help the club's election to the Football League Division Three (South).

The club chairman Harold Walker tried to modernise the club's image by adding AFC and dropping Boscombe Athletic FC in 1972. The aim was to give the team a boost by putting it at the top of any alphabetical list, after the disappointment of relegation to the Fourth Division (League 2) in 1970. However, the plan has failed to elevate the club's status since it is still usually placed between Bolton Wanderers and Bradford City. In 1997 the club adopted the official title of Bournemouth and Boscombe Athletic Community Football Club Limited.

Bournemouth means 'mouth of the stream', from Old English *burna* and *mutha*, in this case a little river that flows through the Pleasure Gardens into the English Channel. Bourne means 'stream', like the Scottish 'burn'.

Nickname: *The Cherries*
The club was nicknamed *The Cherries* in 1910 because of their predominantly red shirts and because their ground was near some cherry orchards.

Ground: *The Fitness First Stadium, Dean Court*
Bournemouth settled at *Dean Court*, then a gravel pit, in 1910 at the invitation of local businessman James E. Cooper Dean, later the club's president, after whom the ground was named. The ground was renamed the *Fitness First Stadium* in a sponsorship deal.

The *Main (West)*, and *North Stand* names are obvious. The *East Stand* used to be the old *Brighton Beach End*, named after the pebbles used to build the original stony bank open terrace and a sarcastic comment on seaside rivals Brighton and Hove Albion and their beach a few miles along the coast.

Crest

The current crest was introduced in the 1970s under the chairman, Harold Walker, who also changed the club's name (see **Club name**, above) and put the players in an AC Milan-style red and black striped kit to give Dean Court a more continental feel. The badge is known as 'Dickie Dowsett's head' in honour of the team's former 1950s centre-forward, one of the club's most prolific scorers, with 79 goals in 169 League games. His head is featured in side profile with flowing locks heading the ball. The shade of red used in the badge is cherry. Dowsett became the club's commercial manager and was an influential figure when it changed its name in 1972 (see above). He was also among the people involved in the crest's design.

Fanzines: *Community Service*, *The 0844 to Waterloo*, *Not the 8502*

Community Service was a post-1997 fanzine named after the club's adoption of its new name (see above). *The 0844 to Waterloo* refers to the train that ferries Bournemouth fans to London when the team are playing away. *Not the 8502* takes its name from the number of extra fans who were attracted to the final few games of the 1987 Third Division (League 1) championship season.

Websites: *Rednblack* (http://bournemouth.rivals.net), *Exiled Cherries* (www.afcbournemouth-mad.co.uk), *Tales from the South End* (www.thesouthend.co.uk)

Rednblack is named after the team colours. *Exiled Cherries* is aimed at exiled Bournemouth fans and also refers to the team nickname, The Cherries (see **Nickname**, above). *Tales from the South End* takes its name from the stand in the old Dean Court (before it was redeveloped) where the hardcore supporters congregated, and from the fact that the original concept of the website was for the fans to send in stories about the team. Over time the website name has been shortened to *The South End*.

Bradford City

In 1903 Manningham Northern Union Rugby Football Club, which was founded in 1876, had mounting financial problems and was encouraged to switch codes from rugby to football. The Football League was so keen to establish football in the West Riding, a Northern Union (later Rugby League) stronghold, that the club, which continued to play at Valley Parade, was accepted into Division Two before it had a team: four days later it became Bradford City.

The Yorkshire town's name means 'broad ford' from Old English *brad* and *ford* and would probably have denoted a ford over what is now the small Bradford Beck River in the city centre.

Nickname: *The Bantams*

The nickname is a reference to the team's claret and amber strip, which resembles the colours of a bantam hen. The birds are small, fast and agile, which it was hoped would represent the team's playing style, though the nickname had unwelcome chicken attributes. In the 1960s, therefore, attempts were made to replace *Bantams* with the *City Gents* (see **Fanzines**, below) or just the *Gents*, although this was not successful (probably because the name suggests a men's lavatory).

Ground: *Valley Parade (The Bradford and Bingley Stadium)*

Manningham Rugby Club, which switched to football and became Bradford City in 1903, first rented the sloping pitch from the Midland Railway Company in 1886. Within a few months the club had turned it into a basic sports ground. *Valley Parade* was adopted from the local street name, which itself was so called because it was next to a steep hill and so could be said to be in a valley. The stadium was renamed under a sponsorship deal with the local Bradford and Bingley Building Society but the supporters still call it Valley Parade.

The *Sunwin (Main) Stand* is named after the sponsors, a local department store. The *Yorkshire First Midland Road (East) Stand* is named after the adjacent road, which is itself named after the Midland Railway from whom the club rented the ground for many years (see above). It is also named after the Yorkshire First Foundation, a faculty of Leeds Metropolitan University, which has a partnership with City involving a commitment from the university to help the club develop closer links with its communities. In return, the university delivers training courses at the club's new educational centre, providing flexible learning opportunities to individuals, communities and local businesses. The *T.L. Dallas Stand (Bradford End)* is named after the sponsors, an insurance brokers, but it is traditionally known as the *Bradford End* because it is nearest the city. The *Carlsberg Stand (Manningham End)* is named after the Danish brewing company. The stand was originally called *Nunn's Kop* after one of City's founding fathers.

Crest
The crest shows a bantam chicken (see **Nickname**, above).

Fanzine: *City Gent* **(http://bradfordcity.rivals.net)**
The name comes from a 1960s cartoon of a 'City Gent', modelled on a famous Bradford director, dressed in a playing kit with a bowler, brolly and briefcase, who appeared for many years on the cover of the programme. Bradford has always been a city associated with industry, and was wealthy in Victorian times, but by the 1960s the mill owners and the well-off had moved to Harrogate and beyond. There was an attempt to use 'City Gents' as the club's nickname but it failed to stick. Nobody knows why the City Gent came into existence, though it was probably a tongue-in-cheek observation of the city or the club having delusions of grandeur. The City Gent has survived as the Bradford mascot, Lenny, a man in a bowler hat who throws sweets to children in the crowd before matches.

Websites: *The Boy from Brazil* **(www.boyfrombrazil.co.uk),** *Valley Parade View* **(www.valleyparadeview.co.uk),** *Valley of Dreams* **(www.valleyofdreams.co.uk)**
The Boy from Brazil was named after a Brazilian player called Edinho, who played for the team in the late 1990s, to make a point about City's progress from being a parochial club. *Valley Parade View* and *Valley of Dreams* are named after the ground.

Brentford

Members of the local rowing club helped form the team, which started as a small amateur outfit in 1889 after an austere board decreed that an alternative form of exercise be introduced for rowers when the waterways were frozen. A committee was assembled to vote on whether rugby union or football should be played and a three-vote majority chose the latter. The club is named after the town in west London, which is near a ford over the River Brent. *Brent* is a Celtic river name meaning 'holy one'.

Nickname: *The Bees*
J.H. Gittens, Brentford's late nineteenth-century star and affiliate of the local college, Borough Road, unwittingly brought about the nickname when he invited a friend to a match at the club's old ground in Ealing. Borrowing the college's war cry, Gittens' friend shouted 'Buck up, Bs'. The crowd misinterpreted his cry as 'Buck Up, Bees'.

Ground: *Griffin Park*
The ground was leased in 1904 from the brewers Fuller, Smith and Turner, who owned the Griffin pub, and is named after their emblem. A griffin is a mythical creature with an eagle's head and wings and a lion's body. *Griffin Park* was built on the site of an orchard, which was cut down by members of the public, who were allowed to keep the timber.

The stands are called the *Braemar Road (Main) Stand, Brook Road, Ealing Road Terrace* and *New Stand (New Road Terrace)* after the name of local roads.

Crest
The current four-quartered black, red and white crest displays the Middlesex county arms with a beehive diagonally opposite. 'Founded 1889' and 'Football Club' appear in the other two quarters beneath the club name. The crest was introduced in 1993. The first crest, which was very similar to the present design, was introduced in the 1971–2 season.

Fanzines: *Beesotted, Thorne In The Side, Hey Jude*

Beesotted (www.beesotted.com) is a reference to the team's nick-name and the fans' devotion to the club. *Thorne in the Side* was named after Steve Thorne, who played one game for Brentford at Gillingham, scored but never played again. *Hey Jude*, now defunct, was named after the Beatles song, which the team used to run out to in the late 1970s. The song has been re-instated and the team once again enter the field of play to the record.

Websites: *The Beehive* (**www.brentford-mad.co.uk**), *Make it Beesy on Yourself* (**www.makeitbeesy.com**)

The Beehive takes its name from club's nickname (see **Nickname**, above). *Make it Beesy on Yourself* is also a reference to the team's nickname, and a play on the title of the song 'Make It Easy On Yourself' written by Burt Bacharach and Hal David, which was a number one hit for the Walker Brothers. It has been sung by the fans since the 1970s when the original was released. The website's sub-title is 'Because going up is so very hard to do' which is again a play on words, using a line from the song's chorus:

> And make it easy on yourself
> Make it easy on yourself
> 'Cause breaking up is so very hard to do.

When the website was launched at the start of the 2003–4 season, following Brentford's sixteenth-place finish in the Second Division (League 1) the previous season, the sub-title was 'Because staying up is so very hard to do'. It seemed appropriate at the time, as they finished one place lower at the end of that campaign and the fans felt football had been anything but easy on them. With the team since pushing for promotion the change to a more optimistic sub-title was deemed appropriate.

Brighton and Hove Albion

Brighton United first played at the Sussex County Cricket Ground in 1898. They were asked to leave in 1900, and Brighton and Hove Rangers were formed in their place, using a field at Home Farm, Withdean. The club was going to be called Brighton and Hove United but local rivals Hove United complained to the FA. Instead, the team's name was changed to Brighton and Hove Albion after the Albion Hotel in Queen's Road where the club members held their committee meetings. Albion is an old-fashioned name for the British Isles, probably derived from the Latin for cliff, *albus*, or the Celtic word for mountain, *alp*. The Victorians frequently attached the word to pub names.

The name of the well-known English resort in East Sussex evolved from the Old English *Beorhthelms tun*, 'Beorhthelm's farm'. The farm owner is not known but his name means 'bright helmet', implying a famous warrior. Brighton, which appears in the Domesday Book as Brighthelmstone or Brithelmeston, after a mythical Bishop of Selsey, was known by this name as recently as the 1800s.

Nicknames: *The Seagulls, The Shrimps, Albion*
Seagulls and *Shrimps* are references to the club's coastal location. The club were officially known as the *Dolphins* until a first round FA Cup match in 1975 at home to their arch-rivals Crystal Palace, known as the *Eagles* (see **Crystal Palace**, Nicknames). A few Palace fans started chanting 'Eagles' in the Bo'sun pub before the match and a group of Brighton supporters, no doubt somewhat embarrassed by their Dolphins nickname, responded with a chant of 'Seagulls'. The club director Derek Chapman is said to have been among the group who first gave the club the nickname. Brighton officially adopted the name and soon incorporated it into their club badge (see **Crest**, below).

Ground: *Withdean Stadium, Goldstone Ground*
Brighton moved to *Withdean*, a council-owned athletics stadium in the Brighton suburb of the same name, on a temporary basis in 1999 after a two-year exile sharing a ground seventy miles away in Gillingham. Their *Goldstone Ground* had been sold for redevelop-

ment in 1997 and turned into a shopping centre. The club hopes to move to a new ground provisionally called the *Falmer Stadium* after the attractive small village between Brighton and Lewes in East Sussex, which is divided by the A27 Brighton bypass (see **Fanzines**, below).

In 1901 Hove FC were offered a perfect place for a ground at Goldstone Bottom, which gets its name from a 20-ton megalith that lay in a field behind where Brighton's West Stand eventually stood and which may have been important to ancient Druids. The large stone was so popular with sightseers and archaeologists that the farmer buried it. It was dug up in 1900 and moved six years later across the road to Hove Park, where it has remained. Hove opened the Goldstone Ground on 7 September, the same day that Albion played under their new name for the first time.

In February 1902 Albion were due to play a home game at the cricket ground but the pitch had already been booked. Hove invited Albion to use the Goldstone and repeated the offer for their next four games until a formal groundshare was agreed in the summer. Two years later Hove sold their lease to Albion and moved back to Hove Park and obscurity.

The *North* and *South Stand* names are obvious, the Elwood Avenue end is unnamed and the other end of the ground is undeveloped.

Crest

The current crest was introduced in 1998 following a takeover of the troubled south coast club. It shows a white seagull beneath the club name and above 'The Seagulls'. The new chairman, Dick Knight, wanted a fresh start after a difficult period under the previous board that had seen the club taken to the brink of extinction and saw an updated crest as a sign of better times ahead for the club and its supporters.

Fanzines: *One F in Falmer, Seaside Saga, Scars and Stripes, Build A Bonfire*

One F in Falmer is taken from the name of the site on which the club hopes to build a £44 million, 22,000 capacity community stadium. The fanzine is part of the campaign to raise money for a move to the proposed development at Falmer. *Seaside Saga, Scars and Stripes* and *Build A Bonfire* all reflect the disillusionment of the fans with a board, including the majority shareholder Bill Archer and the chief executive David Bellotti, which sold the Goldstone Ground to developers in the mid-1990s, leaving Brighton homeless. *Seaside Saga* refers to the whole sorry story played out by the seaside; *Scars and Stripes* recalls the scars from the affair along with the team's blue and white striped kit; *Build A Bonfire* comes from a terrace song whose lyrics express the deep sense of anger felt by the fans against the board for selling the ground.

Website: *Flying High* **(www.bhafc.cjb.net)**
Flying High is a reference to the club's Seagulls nickname and lofty position in the Second Division (League 1) in March 2002, when it looked certain that they would be promoted. Brighton went up to the First Division (Championship) as champions that year.

Bristol City

The club was formed as Bristol South End in 1894 and adopted the name Bristol City three years later on turning professional.

'Bristol', means 'assembly place by the bridge'. The bridge may have been where Bristol Bridge is now, crossing the Floating Harbour (a waterway network that runs through the southern part of the town and connects with the River Avon). Bristol Bridge was built in 1768 to replace the original bridge of 1247. The final 'l' of the name comes from the local pronunciation.

Nickname: *The Robins*
The Robins is a reference to the team's red strip. The nickname, which became popular in the 1940s, was first used in 1926, when the Harry Woods song 'When the Red, Red Robin Goes Bob, Bob, Bobbing Along' was a hit. A robin appeared on the club's badge from 1976 to 1994.

Ground: *Ashton Gate*
In April 1900 City merged with Bedminster, whose ground at *Ashton Gate* became the club's permanent home in 1904. Ashton Gate is an area of Ashton that takes its name from the point at which the River Avon enters the boundaries of the City of Bristol.

The *GWR Dolman Stand*, opened in 1970, was named after Harry Dolman, who became chairman in 1949 and held the post for over thirty years. Dolman, an engineer who bought out the firm he worked for, designed the first set of floodlights installed at Ashton Gate in the early 1950s. The radio station GWR FM sponsors the family enclosure. The *Prime Time Recruitment (Main) Stand*, formerly called the *Williams Stand* after the City chairman Des Williams, is now named after the sponsors.

The *Atyeo (North) Stand* was opened in 1994 and named after Wiltshire striker John Atyeo, City's greatest player, who scored a club record of 395 goals in 700 matches between 1951 and 1966, when he retired from playing. Peter John Walter Atyeo, born on 7 February 1932, was signed under the noses of League champions Portsmouth in 1951. With his predatory instincts, turn of pace and hunger for goals Atyeo, who was never sent off, attracted offers from

Chelsea, Tottenham Hotspur and Liverpool that would have made him the most expensive player in the country, but he turned them all down. He won six England caps from 1955 to 1957, scoring five goals. He died of a heart attack, aged 61, on 8 June 1993, the year before the stand that replaced the Park End was opened and named in his honour.

The *Wedlock Blackthorn (East) End* was named after City's pre-First World War England defender Billy Wedlock (1880–1965). Wedlock, nicknamed the 'India Rubber Man' and 'Fatty Wedlock', played twenty-six times for England between 1907 and 1914 and is considered by most City fans to be the club's second greatest player after John Atyeo (see above). Born on 28 October 1880, William John Wedlock, a centre-half whose skill outweighed his short, stout stature, played for City from 1900 to 1901 and from 1905 until he retired in 1921. Towards the end of his playing career he started running a pub called the Star opposite the ground's main entrance on Ashton Road. It was renamed Wedlock's in his honour after his death on 25 January 1965. 'Blackthorn' is taken from the name of the sponsors, Blackthorn Cider, based in Bristol.

Crest
The club badge was introduced in 1897. It is based on the city's coat of arms, which has its origins in the early seals of Bristol. The arms show a golden ship, representing Bristol's seafaring traditions, leaving the watergate of a silver castle, signifying a strongly fortified harbour. The shield was in use from about the fourteenth century. The helmet above the shield symbolises the armies associated with Bristol's early history. The crossed arms above the crown hold the scales of justice in one hand and a green serpent, denoting wisdom, in the other. In 1569 two unicorns were added as supporters.

Fanzine: *One Team In Bristol*
One Team In Bristol is a reference to the fact that Bristol City were the only League team playing in Bristol while Bristol Rovers shared non-League Bath City's Twerton Park ground from 1986 to 1996 (see **Bristol Rovers**, Ground).

Website: *Over the Gate* (**www.bristolcity-mad.co.uk**)
Over the Gate is a reference to the club's ground at Ashton Gate.

Bristol Rovers

The club was formed in 1883 by a group of schoolteachers. Since they were originally based at Purdown they were known as the Purdown Poachers until the players got a set of black shirts and became the Black Arabs, after the Arabs rugby team that played on an adjoining pitch. The club was renamed Eastville Rovers in 1884 and Bristol Eastville Rovers in 1897. It adopted its present name in 1898. (For origins of the name 'Bristol', see **Bristol City**).

Nicknames: *The Pirates, The Gas, Black Arabs*
Pirates reflects the city's seafaring heritage and may have originated from the ship shown on the Bristol coat of arms, which reflect the city's prominence as one of Britain's major ports at the height of the slave trade and later during the industrial revolution. The coat of arms was once used as the club's badge.

The Gas originates from the Stapleton Gasworks, which used to stand next to the club's old Eastville Stadium. Indeed, most Rovers supporters walked through the gasworks to get to the ground. There are various stories about the benefits of the smell. One is that Rovers were losing heavily in a match and, coincidentally, at halftime the gasworks fired up. The team came out for the second half and won. Some supporters claimed that the fumes had put the team on a high. Another story suggests that when the heads of the gasometers were rising the smell from the fumes that wafted over the stadium over-came the opposition and helped Rovers win. It was, however, Bristol City supporters who originally branded Rovers fans as Gasheads and the club as The Gas. Since the names were not particularly offensive (the equivalent terms for City supporters were Shitheads and The Shit) the Rovers fans adopted them as their own during the club's exile at Twerton Park.

Black Arabs is taken from the club's name in the 1880s.

Ground: *The Memorial Stadium*
Bristol Rugby Football Club's *Memorial Ground*, which is just a mile from the soccer club's old *Eastville Stadium*, became Rovers' home in 1996. The move soccer to the Memorial followed a spell at Twerton Park, where there was a ground-sharing agreement with

non-League Bath City. This had begun in 1986, after Rovers had left Eastville following a fire and disagreements with the landlords. The present stadium is a memorial to the First World War – the biggest war memorial in Bristol.

The *DAS (West) Stand* takes its name from an insurance company based in Bristol. The *Hill House Hammond (Centenary) Stand* was named after the rugby club's centenary in 1990 (Rovers' centenary was in 1983). Hill House Hammond is an insurance company. The *Blackthorn End*, which used to be known as the *Clubhouse End* because of the rugby clubhouse, is named after the sponsors, Blackthorn Cider, a company based in Bristol.

Crest

The crest shows a pirate, which was introduced on the badge in 1997 and is taken from the club's nickname 'The Pirates' (see **Nicknames**, above). He replaced an abstract design of interlocking squares, which had itself replaced the coat of arms of Bristol.

Fanzines: *The Second Of May, Black Arab*

The Second of May (www.geocities.com/Colosseum/Stadium/ 4720/main.html) was the day Rovers beat Bristol City in 1990 to clinch promotion and deny their arch-rivals the Third Division (now League 1) title. The fanzine began life as *Nine and a Half Months* in 1989 but things changed the following year when a momentous event took place in Bath on 2 May at Twerton Park. Rovers were hosting City in a game that would decide the Third Division championship. If City won they were champions while a draw would guarantee promotion. If Rovers won they would be promoted. Rovers secured a 3-0 victory and went on to win the title with City promoted as runners-up. The fanzine decided the event should not be forgotten and changed its name to the date of the game.

Black Arab (www.blackarab.co.uk) is a reference to the club's nickname in the early 1880s (see **Nicknames**, above).

Website: *Goodnight Irene* (www.sportnetwork.net/main/ s128php)

Goodnight Irene is named after the club's anthem. At the same time as Rovers were being formed in 1883 'Goodnight Irene' was being penned in the deep south of the United States. The first transcript appeared in the 1800s but the version known today was originally written and sung in the 1930s by the legendary blues singer Huddie

Leadbetter, better known as Leadbelly.

There have been about forty versions of the song, and the club has four recordings of different renditions. Rovers fans first sang along to it when Frank Sinatra's version reached number one in the UK in 1950. Because the River Frome ran alongside the club's Eastville ground, they readily identified with two lines in particular when the team lost: 'Sometimes I have a great notion, / To jump in the river and drown'.

However, 'Irene' was never really sung that much until the club's exile at Twerton Park from 1986. It became especially popular after the first team squad released a single in the 1990 Third Division Championship year when Rovers also reached the Leyland Daf Cup final at Wembley. Since then the song has taken on more prominence: everyone joins in singing it at matches, and a version by the Five Smith Brothers is regularly played at home games.

Burnley

The club was founded in 1881 by members of the disbanded Burnley Rovers rugby team, who switched to football the following year. They dropped 'Rovers' from their name during a meeting at the Bull Hotel.

'Burnley' means 'woodland clearing by the River Brun', from the Old English river name *brun*, 'brown', and *burna*, 'stream'.

Nickname: *The Clarets*
The nickname is a reference to the colour of the team's strip.

Ground: *Turf Moor*
The ground was literally a square of turf on the moors when the club began playing there in 1883.

The *Bob Lord Stand* is named after the club's controversial former chairman (from 1955), although locals dubbed it the Martin Dobson Stand because the midfielder's £300,000 transfer fee from Everton in August 1974 was said to have paid most of the building costs of £450,000.

Lord was an abrasive local butcher who was credited with transforming the club into one of the top English teams of the 1960s, with a first class stadium. He looked like a 1930s footballer but loved everything modern, including arranging for the team to fly to away games. He engineered Burnley's ascendancy on and off the pitch. Ignoring his fellow directors he bought eighty acres of farmland for an advanced training centre at Gawthorpe. Burnley set up a youth scheme that quickly became the envy of much bigger clubs. Lord was also determined to modernise Turf Moor with a new Cricket Field Stand (see below). The new Bob Lord Stand was opened by the former Prime Minister and Conservative Party leader Edward Heath, a personal friend of Lord's, on 14 September 1974. Lord, who was a vice-president of the Football League, died in 1981 when he was acting president, just before Burnley's centenary.

The *James Hargreaves (Longside) Stand* is named after a local plumbers' merchants that sponsors the stand. The *Jimmy McIlroy Stand* (formerly the *Bee Hole Terrace* after a former colliery nearby) was named after the club's Northern Ireland striker who was a member of the side that won the League Championship in 1960 and reached the 1962 FA Cup final, which they lost 3–1 to Tottenham Hotspur. McIlroy played in the 1958 World Cup and finished his career with fifty-five caps. He later became a journalist in Lancashire and was included among the Football League Centenary 100 Players. The *Cricket Field (David Fishwick) Stand* was named after the Burnley Cricket Club next door and opened in 1969, although it was not officially unveiled until the Prime Minister Edward Heath opened the stand on 23 November 1973. The sponsor, David Fishwick, is an LDV vans dealer in Colne.

Crest
The current crest was introduced in 1973, so that the club would have an exclusive badge that they could copyright. The red rose is the county symbol of Lancashire, the bee represents the area's busy industries, the shuttle the old industries and the visor the new. The rampant lions are surrounded by leaves, representing strength, and a hand of friendship.

Fanzine: *Bob Lord's Sausages*
The fanzine is so-called because the club's late chairman Bob Lord was a local butcher (see **Ground**, above).

Website: *The Claret Flag* (www.claretflag.com)
The name comes from the terrace song that ends with the line 'We'll keep the Claret Flag flying high', a reference to the club's colours, based on the old labour movement song, 'The Red Flag'.

Bury

The club was founded during a meeting at the Old White Horse Hotel in Bury in 1885, as the successor to Bury Wesleyans and Bury Unitarians.

The name of the town in Greater Manchester originates in Old English *burh*, a 'fort town', or borough. It means a 'place by the fort or stronghold'.

Motto
Vincit Omnia Industria. Effort Overcomes All.

Nickname: *Shakers*
The name is thought to have originated from a chance remark by the club's upbeat chairman Mr J.T. Ingham at the 1892 Lancashire Cup final. Undaunted by Bury's role as underdogs against Blackburn Rovers, he shouted 'We'll give them a shaking, for we are the Shakers.'

Ground: *Gigg Lane*
Bury have played at *Gigg Lane* since the club was founded in 1885. The ground was part of the Earl of Derby's estate and he gave Gigg Lane to the club in 1922.

The *South Stand (Milliken Enclosure)* is named after the local sponsors, Milliken Carpets. They no longer sponsor the club but the signs advertising the company remain. The *West (Manchester Road End) Stand* is named after Manchester's northern suburbs, which are just three miles away. The *Cemetery End* is named after the nearby cemetery.

Crest
The club badge is the same as the town's coat of arms, which was originally granted in 1877. The arms show an implement representing weaving, surrounded by the symbols of local industries: an anvil (metalwork), a fleece (wool), two shuttles (textiles), and stems of the papyrus plant (papermaking). The club motto 'Effort Overcomes All' is shown at the bottom of the crest.

Fanzines: *The Hatchet, Dead and Bury(ed)*

The Hatchet comes from the expression 'to bury the hatchet'. The saying originates in the North American Indians' belief that when they smoked their peace pipes they were commanded by the Great Spirit to bury their hatchets, scalping knives and war clubs so that all signs of hostility would be out of sight. The custom was referred to in H.W. Longfellow's *Song of Hiawatha* (1855):

> Buried was the bloody hatchet,
> Buried was the dreadful war-club,
> Buried were all warlike weapons,
> And the war-cry was forgotten.
> There was peace among nations.

Dead and Bury(ed) is a play on words.

Website: *y3kshakers* (www.y3shakers.net)

y3kshakers means 'Why (only) three thousand Shakers?' (Since the gates have dropped, this should now be 'Why two and a half thousand Shakers?'!) 'Shakers' is the team's nickname (see **Nickname**, above).

Cardiff City

The club was formed in 1899 by members of the Riverside Cricket Club; Albion was added to the name in 1902. Cardiff became a city in 1905 and three years later the local FA gave the club permission to change its name to Cardiff City.

The name of the capital city of Wales is an Anglicisation of Caerdydd, 'fort on the Taff', from the Welsh *caer*, 'fort', and the name of the river on which Cardiff stands, the Taff, which itself probably means 'water'.

Nickname: *The Bluebirds*
The nickname is a reference to the team's blue strip.

Ground: *Ninian Park*
In 1910 the local council granted Cardiff a seven-year lease on the ground, a rubbish tip provisionally named *Sloper Park* after nearby Sloper Road, provided there were guarantees for the £90 a year rent. When one of the club's backers pulled out, Lord Ninian Crichton Stuart, who shortly afterwards became MP for Cardiff, acted as guarantor and Sloper Park became *Ninian Park*. Ninian himself kicked off the first match against the League champions Aston Villa on 1 September. He died in action in the trenches in 1915, during the First World War.

The *Grange End* was formerly the Grangetown terrace or *Grangemouth End*. The *Popular Bank Stand* is also known as the *Bob Bank* because fans used to pay a bob (slang for an old shilling, 5p today) to get in. The *Canton Stand* is named after the nearby district of Canton.

At the time of writing, the club plans to move to a new 30,000 capacity stadium at Leckwith as part of a £40 million project.

Crest
The Bluebird is the club's nickname and a reference to the team's colours (see **Nickname**, above).

Fanzines: *The Thin Blue Line, Ramzine, Watch the Bluebirds Fly, O Bluebird of Happiness*
The Thin Blue Line is the title of a television sitcom set in a police station; blue is the link to Cardiff. *Ramzine* is a reference to Welsh sheep. *Watch the Bluebirds Fly* and *O Bluebird of Happiness* refer to the team's nickname.

Websites: *Valley Rams* (www.valleyrams.com), *A Sleeping Giant* (www.ccfcsleepinggiant.com), *Bluebirds Online* (www.bluebirdsonline.com), *Blue Madness* (www.bluemadness.co.uk), *Bluebird to the Bone* (www.sportnetwork.net/main/s120.php), *1927 Club* (www.1927club.com)
Valley Rams is a supporter's group set up to provide coaches for City fans from the Welsh valleys. *A Sleeping Giant* was named when City, potentially a big club, were languishing in the Third Division in the mid to late 1990s. *Bluebirds Online, Blue Madness (The Nutty Sounds of Cardiff City)* and *Bluebird to the Bone* refer to the team nickname (see **Nickname**, above). *1927 Club* is named after Cardiff's famous FA Cup final success in that year, when a 1–0 victory over Arsenal took the Cup outside England for the first and so far only time. The victorious team contained only three Welshmen, one Englishman, three Scots and four Irishmen. The name reflects the fact that the website is run by the London and south-east England branch of the Cardiff City Supporters Club.

Carlisle United

The club was formed in 1903 when two Carlisle-based teams, Shaddongate United and Carlisle Red Rose, merged.

The north-west town's name is derived from the old Celtic *cair*, 'fortified town', together with the name of the Roman fort itself, 'Luguvalium', from the personal name Luguvallos, meaning 'strong as Lugus', a Celtic god. *Cair* was added after the Roman period, during which Hadrian's Wall was constructed.

Motto
Unita Fortior. Forever United.

Nicknames: *The Cumbrians, Blues*
The Cumbrians is a reference to the team's location in the county town of Cumbria and its status as the largest city. *Blues* refers to the colour of the team's strip.

Ground: *Brunton Park*
The club moved to *Brunton Park* in 1909 after they had been ordered to leave their previous ground at Devonshire Park by the Duke of Devonshire's estate. The original five-acre site bordering the Warwick Road rugby ground was in an area that may have been known as Bunting Meadows in the 1800s; the name evolved into Brunton over the years.

The *East Stand (Scratching shed)* was also known as the *Popular side* or *Scratchers*. The *Warwick Road End* is named after the nearby road. The *Petterill (Waterworks) End* is named after the River Petteril that runs not far behind. It is also known as the *Waterworks End* because there used to be a waterworks called Stony Holme pumping station behind it, on the site now occupied by a golf course and club-house.

Crest
The badge is the same as the city's coat of arms, which was registered in 1924. The red cross on gold is thought to have been the family arms of Sir William de Carlyell of Cumberland. The red roses in the corner were the symbols of the Virgin Mary, patron saint of

the priory of Carlisle, of which the cathedral was a part. The gold rose in the centre is the badge of King Edward I. Above the arms is a distinctive crown representing the town's castle, whose massive Norman keep is one of the best of its kind in England. Construction of the castle was begun in 1092 by William Rufus but it has been altered many times during more than 900 years of military use. It stands on the site of a Celtic hill-fort at the apex of the town walls at the north-west end of the city guarding the English-Scottish border and its own walls were once joined to the city walls. It served as a prison for Mary Queen of Scots. The gateway reflects the fact that the town was an ancient border fortress about ten miles from Scotland. Two wyverns support the arms, mythical half-dragon, half-serpent creatures similar to a dragon, except that wyverns cannot breathe fire and have only two legs. They were included to represent the ancient connection between Celtic Wales (Cymru) and Celtic Cumbria, whose names both refer to the *cymry*, or 'fellow countrymen'. A red dragon supports the arms of Cumbria County Council for the same reason. The motto, 'Be just and fear not', is a line spoken by Cardinal Thomas Wolsey in Act 3 Scene 2 of Shakespeare's play *Henry VIII*.

Fanzines: *Olga the Fox, So Jack Ashurst, where's my shirt?, Watching from the Warwick, Land of Sheep and Glory, Cumberland Sausage*

Olga the Fox refers to United's mascot. For thirty-four years Olga was paraded before matches by a local dustman, George Baxter, nicknamed Twinkletoes, who was always smartly dressed in a blue and white top hat and tails. When Baxter died in the early 1980s the red fox was retired. Olga's stuffed remains are on display in a glass case in the club's entrance lobby.

So Jack Ashurst, where's my shirt? is a reference to a shirt promised to one of the fanzine editors after a crucial match by one-time Carlisle player Jack Ashurst. *Watching from the Warwick* is a reference to the Warwick Road End terrace, and *Land of Sheep and Glory* is a play on the title of the hymn 'Land of Hope and Glory' and a joke about Cumbrians and sheep. *Cumberland Sausage* is a reference to the famous locally-made sausage. Cumberland roughly corresponds with the present-day county of Cumbria.

Websites: *94th minute.com* (www.94thminute.com), *Reeves is offside again!* (www.kynson.org.uk), *3 Games in Hand* (www.angelfire.com/dc/3games)

94th minute refers to the timing of goalkeeper Jimmy Glass's last-gasp goal against Plymouth Argyle which preserved Carlisle's league status on the last day of the 1998–9 season. The on-loan goalkeeper sprinted from his goal line and arrived late in the penalty area for a corner kick. Scott Dobie's flashing header was parried by the Plymouth keeper straight to the feet of Glass, who fired home the injury-time winner that saw Scarborough relegated to the Conference instead of United, in one of the most dramatic ends to a season anyone had seen. The goal sparked a pitch invasion by United fans. After three or four minutes the referee blew the whistle to restart the game and immediately signalled the end of the match. United were safe!

Striker David Reeves was Carlisle's captain when Dave Atkinson started the *Reeves is offside again!* website. Reeves was always being caught offside; even his nickname was 'You're offside'. He was the club's record buy when he arrived in 1993 from Notts County for £121,000 and scored 63 goals in 168 appearances, including 11 in 36 games in his first season.

When *3 Games in Hand* started in January 2001, Carlisle were stuck at the bottom of the Third Division (now League 1) table. They were six points adrift but had three games in hand over their fellow strugglers. A fine team effort over the second half of the season left Carlisle safe going into the final game, something that had looked impossible just a few months earlier.

Charlton Athletic

The club was formed in 1905 by teenagers living near the River Thames, in the area that now borders the Thames Barrier. The London club takes it name from the district in the south-east of the city called Charlton, a common place name that usually means 'farmstead of the freemen or peasants'.

Nicknames: *(H)addicks, Valiants, The Robins*
Haddicks, or *Addicks*, from 'haddock', is believed to date from as long ago as 1908 when the players used a room over Arthur Bryan's fishmonger's shop in East Street (now Eastmoor Street) as their base, close to a pub called 'The Lads of the Village'. The players loved haddock and chips and supposedly treated their opponents to a fish supper after matches. The shop owner was a keen fan who went to games carrying a haddock nailed to a piece of wood, which he waved around during matches. The now defunct *Kentish Independent* used the nickname 'The Haddocks' in its Charlton match reports in 1908. Its coverage of the Woolwich Cup final win over New Beckton in 1910 said 'several large haddocks from Mr Arthur Bryan's shop were paraded around the ground on poles.' Bryan died in 1956 aged 74. Other theories are that many of the club's original supporters worked in the fish markets, or that the word is a south-east London form of 'addict', meaning 'fan'. In 1946 Eddie Marshall and the club secretary, Harry Hughes, who were at Charlton as player and committee member respectively in the 1905–6 season, insisted that 'Addicks' was a corruption of 'Athletic'. In those early years it was a junior club with a strong following among children who shouted 'Up the Addicks' because they found it hard to pronounce 'Up the Athletic'.

The team were also known as the *Robins* after the colour of the team strip. The Royal Artillery Band used to play 'The Red, Red, Robin' as the team ran on to the pitch, a song still used today. The nickname *Valiants* was adopted in 1963 from a list of suggestions by the club's development association to link where Charlton played, The Valley, to their new crest (see **Crest**, below). Despite the use of these other nicknames the fans still referred to the club as the Addicks. When the headline 'The Telly Addicks' was used for a story in the local *Mercury* newspaper about the new ITV television contract covering the Football League at the start of the 1988–9 season it started the revival of the Addicks nickname.

Ground: *The Valley*

Charlton began building their home ground in 1919 in an old sand and chalk pit, known locally as 'the Swamp', after local fans had helped to raise the money to buy the site. Volunteers cleared the area and dug out the pitch. To form banked terraces at either end earth, containing many bones, was brought in from a local hospital excavation. It looked like a valley after the excavations to turn it into a football pitch were completed.

West and *North (Covered End) Stand* names are obvious, while the *East Stand* was formerly called the *Mound, Cliff* or *East Bank*. The *Jimmy Seed (South) Stand* was named in 1981 after the club's successful manager. Seed, in charge from 1933 to 1956, led Charlton from the Third to the First Division (now Premier League) in successive seasons and in 1937 they finished runners-up. Under Seed Charlton also won the FA Cup in 1947 beating Burnley 1–0 in extra time after finishing runners-up the previous year to Derby County, who won 4–1, again after an extra period. Seed was the longest-serving manager in the Football League until he was overtaken by Manchester United's Matt Busby.

The *Sam Bartram Gates*, at the main entrance to the *Valley* and Sam Bartram Close on the small estate next to a 1970s tower block called Valiant House, are named after Charlton's late goalkeeper, who played for the club from 1934 to 1956. Born in Simonside, County Durham, the most celebrated player in Addicks' history was a fanatical Newcastle United fan. But Bartram, who started out as a wing-half then switched to centre-forward, was spotted by the brother of Charlton's Whitburn-born manager Jimmy Seed playing a blinder as an emergency goalkeeper in a local cup final replay that finished 0–0 in 1934. Within weeks Charlton offered the Bolden Villa player a two-week trial.

The club wasn't immediately impressed as Bartram, who also worked as a coal miner, conceded eight goals in two reserve games. But Seed saw something in the likeable 20-year-old and he was offered a second chance. By Christmas he had made his first-team debut and two decades later one of the finest goalkeepers of his generation was still playing for his adopted club. He inspired Charlton to their 1947 FA Cup success, after suffering defeat in the final the previous year, and his 623 appearances in 21 years remains the club's record. Known as the finest goalkeeper never to play for England, in the era of Frank Swift and Bert Williams, he did however play in three wartime internationals. He was runner-up to Tom Finney for Footballer of the Year at the age of 40 in 1956. Bartram died aged 67 in 1981.

Crest
The crest, showing a hand holding a sword, was chosen as the winner of a competition held by the club in 1963. The winning entry was based on a local coat of arms from the Spencer-Percival family, prominent figures in late nineteenth-century south London. After numerous alterations, including the addition of a surrounding ring and the club name, the current crest was first used for a derby against Millwall on August 10 1968.

Fanzines: *Voice of the Valley, Valley Floyd Road, Goodbye Horse*
Voice of the Valley was launched in February 1988 as a rallying point to guide fans through the complex financial, political and planning issues related to the campaign for a return to The Valley, which the club had left in 1985. The fanzine's campaign gave the fans a voice in the debate. *Valley Floyd Road* is a supporters' song that goes to the tune of Paul McCartney's 'Mull of Kintyre'.

> Valley Floyd Road, the mist rolling in from the Thames,
> My desire, is always to be found at Valley Floyd Road.
> Many miles have I travelled, many games have I seen,
> Following Charlton my favourite team,
> Many hours have I spent in the Covered End choir,
> Singing Valley Floyd Road, my only desire...

The song takes its title from the club's ground, since the main entrance to The Valley is on Floyd Road.

Goodbye Horse was named after a supporters' song about a policeman who came off his horse and had to chase it down the road at a Charlton match in the 1970s: 'Goodbye horse, goodbye horse / Saying goodbye to his horse'.

Websites: *Addicks Online* (www.addicksonline.co.uk) *Net Addicks* (http://charltonathletic.rivals.net)
Addicks Online and *Net Addicks* refer to the club nickname (see **Nicknames**, above).

Chelsea

In 1904 Gus Mears hatched a plan to build a stadium on the land he owned at Stamford Bridge. When Fulham were considering moving from Craven Cottage he asked the club if it wanted to use the stadium but the chairman, Henry Norris, turned him down. Mears decided to form a new club in 1905. Several names were suggested, including Stamford Bridge, Kensington and London FC, but Mears' friend Fred Parker chose Chelsea after the south-west central London district that had just been designated a Royal Borough by Edward VII. The Chelsea Football and Athletic Company was thus launched in May 1905.

'Chelsea' actually means 'chalk landing place' from Old English *cealc*, 'chalk' and *hyth*, 'landing place', denoting a place on the River Thames where chalk or limestone was unloaded. The latter part of the district's name has been distorted to suggest 'sea'.

Nickname: *The Blues*
The nickname is a reference to the team's blue strip.

Ground: *Stamford Bridge*
The ground is named after a bridge, once a canal bridge, that went across the now defunct Chelsea railway near the stadium's main entrance. The name 'Stamford' is derived from Sandford, 'the sandy ford'. The original ford, over a small tributary of the Thames at Chelsea Creek, was superseded by a bridge carrying the main road from Chelsea to Fulham – the present King's Road.

The stands are called *North*, *South*, *East* and *West* although the South is sponsored by Umbro and was the *Shed Stand*, while the North has been renamed in memory of former director Matthew Harding (see below).

The *Umbro South Shed Stand* was named after the sportswear company that sponsors the stand. The cover put over the rear of the Fulham Road terracing in 1935 was later referred to as the *Shed* and became a popular standing area for the hardcore home fans. The cover was originally put up for bookmakers on greyhound nights after the Bridge was leased to the Stamford Bridge Stadium Limited, which was set up to run the racing. The roof was old-fashioned, sat awkwardly at the back and was too small to provide a real benefit – hence the nickname. The Shed was taken down in the summer of 1994 when a new South Stand was built.

The *Matthew Harding (North) Stand* was named after the late Matthew Harding, a long-standing supporter, a director of the club and eventually the landlord. Harding's financial involvement with Chelsea began in June 1994 when he answered an advertisement in the *Financial Times* placed by the then-chairman Ken Bates asking for potential investors to contact the club. He was born in Haywards Heath, Sussex on 26 December 1953, the son of a Lloyd's under-writer, and was educated at Abingdon School Oxford, which he left, disappointed, with just one A level, in Latin. Harding decided to follow in his father's footsteps and in 1973, at the age of 19, he became an apprentice at Ted Benfield's re-insurance brokerage, working within the Lloyd's insurance market. He worked his way up from office clerk to become chairman of the Benfield insurance group. Harding organised a management buyout of the company in 1988 and set about making it the market's most profitable broker. In 1995 his salary was reported to be £3.25 million. At this time Ken Bates was earning £120,000 from Chelsea. Various sources ranked Harding among Britain's hundred richest individuals, with a fortune estimated at £125–170 million.

Harding had been a regular at the Bridge since the age of 8; it was said that he had even met his wife Ruth under the Shed. Harding agreed to contribute £5 million towards a new North Stand in loan stock, joined the board and invested another £2.5 million on players. He was a man of the people and the fans looked on him as one of their own who had simply swapped the terraces for the boardroom. Ever-popular with the crowds, he drank his pre-match Guinness wearing a team shirt alongside fellow supporters in the Imperial Arms in the King's Road. However, relations with Bates became strained when Harding, who owned 27 per cent of the club, paid £16.5 million to buy the ground's leasehold from the Royal Bank of Scotland. Their long-running feud, which was resolved in a some-what uneasy truce only six months before Harding's tragic death, was, as he saw it, a battle for the 'soul' of the club. Bates wanted a futuristic stadium with slick corporate facilities; Harding just dreamed of a brilliant team. By that time, Harding no longer had his seat on the board but he became vice-chairman, retained a 28.5 per cent stake in the company and was chairman of Chelsea Village, the club's parent company.

The 42-year-old was flying back to London on 22 October 1996 after watching Chelsea lose a League Cup tie at Bolton Wanderers when the hired helicopter crashed in Middlewich, Cheshire. Harding died, along with four others, leaving three sons and a daughter by his wife, from whom he had separated, and another daughter by his girlfriend Vicky Jaramillo. Chelsea announced soon after his death that the North Stand, which Harding's money had helped to build, would be named after him. 'I was shocked by the news of Matthew's tragic death,' said the then Conservative Prime Minister John Major, a fellow Chelsea fan. 'Chelsea was his passion and he did a huge amount to help the club he loved.' Ironically, Harding had donated £1 million to the Labour Party the previous month. 'This is quite an appalling tragedy and we all feel devastated for his family,' said the Labour leader Tony Blair, who had used the same French-built helicopter after September's Blackpool conference. Bates said: 'His memory is best served by achieving the objectives that he set for the club – in achieving his dream of a world-class team in a world-class stadium.'

Crest

In the early 1980s the then chairman Ken Bates ordered a change in the crest so it could be copyright protected. Fans were asked to come up with a new design, but as nothing suitable was submitted a professional designer was given the job instead. The badge shows a golden lion regardant (looking over its shoulder) surrounded by the letters CFC in royal blue. The lion hails from the coat of arms of the Earl of Cadogan, former Viscount of Chelsea.

Fanzines: *Matthew Harding's Blue and White Army*, *Blues Brothers*, *Curious Blue*

Matthew Harding's Blue and White Army (now the CFCUK fanzine 'virtual' page on the website http://blueandwhitearmy.net) is named after the club's late landlord (see **Ground**, above). *Curious Blue* and *Blues Brothers* take their names from the team colour. The latter refers to the film title.

Cheltenham Town

Cheltenham Town's earliest recorded match was a friendly against Dean Close School in March 1892.

The Gloucestershire town's name is of uncertain origin. The 'ham' comes from Old English *hamm*, meaning 'enclosure' or 'river meadow' by a hill-slope called 'Celte', describing the site of the original settlement by the river Chelt, whose name comes from the town. The first part of the town's name has been linked to the well-known hills in southern central England called the Chilterns, with perhaps a basic sense 'hill' for both. In Cheltenham the reference is to Cleeve Hill, which overlooks the town to the north-west. Alternatively, 'Chelt' may be an Old English personal name, 'Celta'.

Motto
Salubritas et Eruditio. Health and Learning.

Nickname: *The Robins*
The nickname is a reference to the team's red and white striped shirts and the robin on the club crest (see **Crest**, below).

Ground: *Whaddon Road*
The club moved to *Whaddon Road* in 1932.

The stands are *Main (UCAS)*, *Wymans Road (In2Print)*, *Whaddon Road End* and *Prestbury Road End (C&G)*, which are all named after nearby roads. The sponsors are UCAS (Universities and Colleges Admissions Service), whose Rosehill headquarters is opposite Cheltenham Racecourse, In2Print, a local printing and design company, and C&G, the Cheltenham & Gloucester Building Society.

Crest
The club crest is identical to that of the town. Its inscription *Salubritas et Eruditio*, 'health and learning', refers to two of the main features of Cheltenham's history.

The health element arises from the spa waters 'discovered' in the eighteenth century. Cheltenham had been just a small market town like any other in the Cotswolds until 1716, when flocks of pigeons around the town's springs drew attention to their qualities. The event is represented on the town's crest by a bird and tree. The blue background at the top of the shield is also symbolic of the spa. The water, which is the only alkaline variety in Britain, was said to cure a number of diseases and Cheltenham became Britain's most popular spa. The seal of fashionable approval was set by George III's visit in 1788 and Cheltenham's popularity was further encouraged by the Duke of Wellington and Princess (later Queen) Victoria. Indeed, during Cheltenham's heyday the royal, the rich and the famous descended in hordes to take the waters, which were said to cure anything from constipation to worms.

The 'learning' part of the inscription and the books featured on the crest are due to the large number of colleges in the area, including the esteemed Ladies' College. Visitors like Lord Byron and Jane Austen first added a literary atmosphere. From the 1830s Cheltenham became a favourite retirement spot for officers who had done colonial duty in the army, navy and East India Company. Their presence contributed to the town's rise as an educational centre. Among its public schools, the Gentlemen's College (1841) and the Ladies' College (1853) enjoy an international reputation.

The cross is that of King Edward the Confessor, who owned much of the land that now forms Cheltenham. The oak tree symbolises Cheltenham's historical and present position as one of Britain's foremost garden towns. The fleece at the top of the crest represents the Cotswold sheep that were bought and sold in Cheltenham in the days when it was a market town.

The crest on the team shirts was replaced by the bird in 1971; thereafter the robin and the bird, and sometimes both, appeared, until the crest was reintroduced in 1992.

Fanzines: *They've Scored Again!*
The title is taken from a radio commentary on Cheltenham's match against Rushden and Diamonds on Easter Sunday 1999. Cheltenham were on their way to winning the Conference, but a lot of fans were locked outside the ground listening to the game on BBC Radio Northamptonshire. Cheltenham had been losing 1–0 but scored twice late in the match to take a 2–1 lead: after the second goal the commentator said: 'Oh, f**k, they've scored again.'

Websites: *Electric Robin* (http://cheltenhamtown.rivals.net), *The Robins Nest* (www.thisengland.freeserve.co.uk/ctafc.htm) Electric Robin and Robins Nest are references to the club's nickname.

Chester City

The club was formed in 1884 through the merger of King's School Old Boys and Chester Rovers. It is named after the city and port in north-west England famous for its medieval tradition of football, whose own name comes from Old English *ceaster*, 'Roman fort', ultimately from Latin *castra* or 'camp'. Chester was referred to in the eighth century as 'Legacaestir', the first part of which represents the Latin *legion*, 'of the legions', although the first part of the name has disappeared. In 1983 the club added 'City' to its name.

Nicknames: *Blues, City*
Blues is a reference to the team's blue and white striped shirts; *City* is from the team's name.

Ground: *The Deva Stadium (Saunders Honda Stadium)*
Chester played their first match at the new £3 million *Deva Stadium* on 25 August 1992. Deva, the Roman name for the fort at Chester, comes from the river Dee on which the city stands. The Latin name Deva was chosen as the result of a club competition. Saunders Honda is the local car dealership that sponsors the stadium.

The stands are simply *North, South, East* and *West*.

Crest
The badge shows a wolf's head looking over a crown on a castle rampart surrounded by a circle of leaves and is an adaptation of the City of Chester's crest.

The wolf's head goes back to Norman times, when William the Conqueror's nephew Hugh d'Avranches was appointed Earl of Chester in 1071. D'Avranches earned the nickname Lupus, Latin for 'Wolf', because he was ruthless and, with the help of many cruel barons, shed a lot of Welsh blood. Much of the country resented their Norman overlords and Chester was the last place to be subdued by William's army. The Earl therefore needed to be tough. Although the Prince of Wales now has the honorary title Earl of Chester, the Grosvenor family have since adopted the name Lupus – until the late 1990s Gerald Grosvenor, the Duke of Westminster, was patron of the football club. There used to be a Wolf Gate in the walls of

Chester but it collapsed on the eve of the Second World War and has been replaced by the New Gate.

The crown on the badge may indicate loyalty to the sovereign, since Chester held out for the Royalist cause during the English Civil War. The leaves could be a laurel, as in a victor's crown, or oak leaves, since the oak has a more local significance to Chester, where the tree is commonly found. The oak leaf has also been the symbol of the Cheshire regiment since they saved the life of King George III while he was standing beneath an oak tree at the battle of Dettingen in 1749.

Website: *Early Doors* (http://earlydoors.homestead.com/Home.html)

The website name comes from the common expression 'early doors', meaning near the beginning of a match, which was popularised by the ITV summariser Ron Atkinson. The phrase was used by travelling Chester fans to indicate that they would gather at the nearest pub to an away ground. The website editor Arthur Rutter recalls how on one trip to Mansfield Town the fans agreed to meet 'early doors' at a pub that none of them could remember the name of. 'We parked up at the ground and walked over to the pub, which was actually named "The Early Doors"!'

Chesterfield

Chesterfield can be traced back to a side called Chesterfield Town formed in 1866. The name of the Derbyshire town means 'fort in a field', from Old English *ceaster*, the term for a Roman fort, and *feld*, 'field' or 'open land'.

Nicknames: *Blues, Spireites*
Blues is a reference to the team colours. *Spireites* comes from the crooked spire on the parish church, the fourteenth-century St Mary and All Saints, which dominates the town. It was finished in about 1360 and is the largest in Derbyshire. There are a number of stories about how the spire became crooked. Legend tells of a powerful magician who persuaded a Bolsover blacksmith to shoe the Devil. Unfortunately, he drove a nail into the Devil's foot. Howling with rage and pain, the Devil fled to Chesterfield. Skimming over the church, he lashed out in agony, caught the spire and twisted it out of shape. Another story is that Lucifer sat on the church and spitefully let his massive weight crush its elegant spire. Lucifer, which means 'light-bearer', was the former archangel whose 'fall from grace' is referred to in the Bible: 'How art though fallen from heaven, O Lucifer, son of the morning!' (Isaiah 14.12).

The truth is less fanciful and is probably linked to the ravages of the Black Death, which spread across Britain in the fourteenth century when the church was being built. Many people died in the Plague, among them skilled craftsmen. The survivors built the spire out of timber which, over the years, has become twisted beneath the heavy lead covering.

Ground: *Recreation Ground, Saltergate*
Chesterfield were playing at the *Recreation Ground* in about 1880 before leaving for a few seasons and returning permanently by at least 1887. *Saltergate* is the name of the main thoroughfare at the Spion Kop End. The name recalls the salt merchants who either sold their goods on the road or travelled along it. It may have been the road used by men carrying salt south from Cleveland, where it was mined.

The *Cross Street End* is named after the street that runs behind the stand, which is itself named after the cross of St Mary's School across the road from the ground. For *Spion Kop* see **Liverpool**, Ground section. The *Compton Street Terrace (Popular Side)* is named after the street that runs behind the stand.

Crest

The current crest is a shield with the interlocking initials 'CFC' circled by the words 'Chesterfield F.C. Est., 1866'. It was first introduced in 1946 when the club's colours were changed from blue and white stripes to a plain blue shirt but disappeared in the early 1960s. It was re-introduced after the fanzine *The Crooked Spireite* produced a CFC shield enamel badge that proved popular.

Fanzines: *The Crooked Spireite, Tora Tora Tora, Far and Beyond the Call of Duty*

The title *The Crooked Spireite* was chosen by its former editor Stuart Basson 'because it contains the long-standing club nickname and I thought the "crooked" part would suggest the unofficial status of the fanzine. There was a touch of intentional self-deprecation on my part in naming it after the only thing that the town is famous for.'

The Crooked Spireite ceased publication after the 1997 FA Cup semi-final, which Chesterfield lost to Middlesbrough, but two new fanzines appeared. *Tora Tora Tora* means 'attack, attack, attack', something the fans felt Chesterfield did not do enough under manager John Duncan. *Far and Beyond the Call of Duty* was a comment made by Sky Sports analyst Andy Gray about Chesterfield captain Sean Dyche during the 1997 FA Cup semi-final.

Websites: *Spirezine* (www.spirezine.co.uk), *Compton Street* (www.chesterfield-mad.co.uk)

Spirezine is a combination of the club's nickname and 'fanzine'. *Compton Street* is named after the Compton Street terrace (see **Ground**, above).

Colchester United

Colchester United was formed in 1937 as the successor to an amateur team called Colchester Town, established in 1873.

The first part of the name probably comes from the River Colne on which the ancient Essex town stands. The river's own name is of Celtic origin and means 'water'. Another theory is that 'Colchester' is based on a shortened version of the Latin word *colonia,* a Roman colony for retired legionaries. Its Romano-British name was *Colonia Camulodunum Camulos* meaning a fort, associated with a Celtic war-god. The second part of the name, 'chester' shows it was a Roman camp, from Old English *ceaster.*

Nickname: *The U's*
The nickname is taken from the second word of the club's name.

Ground: *Layer Road*
Layer Road was used by the 4th Battalion King's Royal Rifle Corps, who were stationed at the Colchester garrison in 1906. When the battalion moved in 1909, Colchester Town took their place and three years later bought the ground, which is named after the road leading to Layer-de-la-Haye, known locally as Layer. 'Layer', a name shared with other settlements along the road, is derived from *leire or leyer,* Norse words meaning 'mud'.

The stands are *Main Stand,* the *Clock End, Layer Road End* and *Barside,* also variously known over the years as the *Popular Side, Barn* or *Cowshed.*

The club is currently planning a new 10,000 capacity all-seater Community Stadium as part of a major leisure development at *Cuckoo Farm.*

Crest
The golden eagle on the badge, introduced for the 1972–3 season, was inspired by the town's occupation by the Romans, whose legions carried an eagle emblem. The current crest, introduced in 1994, is the club's fifth, with the imperial eagle set inside a shield against a background of the team's colours of blue and white stripes.

Coventry City

The club was formed in 1883 as the works team of Singer's, who had made bicycles since 1876 and later branched out into manufacturing cars. In 1898 it changed its name from Singer's FC to Coventry City.

The name of the Midlands city means 'Cofa's tree'. Nobody knows who Cofa was or where his tree stood but it was probably a meeting place or marker. Coventre, the Couentrev of the Domesday Book, may derive from a Saxon convent.

Nickname: *Sky Blues*
The nickname is a reference to the colour of the team's strip.

Ground: *The Ricoh Arena*
The club's new *Ricoh Arena* stadium is on the site of a former gasworks at Foleshill. The £60 million, 32,500 all-seater stadium, part of a £113 million scheme including a retail development, exhibition halls, a concert venue and a railway station, is owned by the council and leased back to the club. Ricoh, the eighth largest information technology company in the world, signed a £10 million sponsorship deal to secure the international naming rights for the Arena.

The stands are called *Coventry Evening Telegraph (North)*, *Jewson (South)*, *Marconi (West)* and *NTL (East)* after the sponsors. Jewson is a building materials supplier. Marconi is a telecommunications network provider. NTL is a broadband internet, cable TV and telephone services company which sponsored the Kop stand at the club's old Highfield Road ground (see **Liverpool**, Ground). Highfield Road, named after one of several small residential streets nearby, was sold for housing redevelopment after the club's decision in 1998 to move.

Crest
The badge shows a football with an eagle on the left and a phoenix on the right, on top of which is an elephant with Coventry Castle on its back. The castle was built in the eleventh century by Ranulf Meschines, the Earl of Chester. It was seized by King Stephen and

eventually fell into ruins in the mid-twelfth century. Stone from the castle may have been used to construct other buildings in the town, and the city wall. Mary Queen of Scots was imprisoned in Caesar's tower, the only part of the castle that was not too decayed to house her, and the only portion that still exists, as part of St Mary's Guildhall. It may originally have been the castle gatehouse. The rest of the site has been built over although Bayley Lane is assumed to follow the line of the castle's outer fortifications.

The elephant represents strength and is a symbol of St George, who was believed to have lived in the area, although research shows that he may never have even been in England, let alone Coventry. The city included the elephant in its crest in the nineteenth century and when the football club changed its name from Singer's FC in 1898 it decided to put the elephant on its own badge. The city has since changed its crest and it is now only the Sky Blues who keep St George's memory alive. The eagle represents Lord Leofric, who was married to Lady Godiva (see **Fanzines**, below), and the phoenix rising from the flame is included in memory of those who died in Coventry during the Second World War blitz. A German air raid devastated the old cathedral, much of the city centre and many factories on the night of 14 November 1940.

Fanzines: *Gary Mabbutt's Knee, Twist and Shout, Lady Godiva Rides Again, Peeping Tom*

Gary Mabbutt's Knee (http://coventrycity.rivals.net) is named after the Tottenham Hotspur defender who deflected a cross from Lloyd McGrath into his own goal six minutes into extra time to give Coventry a famous 3–2 victory in the 1987 FA Cup final at Wembley. It was Coventry's first FA Cup final and remains the only major trophy the club has ever won. The fanzine is intended as an affectionate tribute to Gary Mabbutt – one of the finest players in the English game – and to the Cup-winning Coventry City team, who are all heroes to Sky Blues supporters. *Twist and Shout* gets its name from the song which the City fans have sung for years:

> S**t on The Villa
> City till I die
> You are my City, my only City, you make me happy.
> Twist and shout.

Coventry's practical history begins with the foundation of a Benedictine priory in 1043 by Lord Leofric, the 'grim' Earl of

Mercia, and his wife Godgyfu (Godiva). The legend of how Lady Godiva averted her husband's anger from the town by riding naked through its streets gave rise to the fanzine title, *Lady Godiva Rides Again*. The most popular version of the story is that Leofric's beautiful wife was appalled by the poverty she saw and begged her husband to abolish the crippling taxes he levied on his people. Wearying of his wife's nagging, Leofric agreed to do as she asked if she rode naked through the town at noonday. He did not expect a woman of her rank to agree to such a proposal. But Lady Godiva cleverly got around the dilemma by ordering the townsfolk to lock themselves in their houses and bolt their windows on the appointed day. Only one local lad, Peeping Tom (hence another fanzine name), dared to disobey the Countess's command. He bored a hole in his shutters and was struck blind before he had a chance to see Godiva, whose long hair covered her body like a cape as she rode through the city with her eyes lowered. Once the ordeal was over, Godiva returned to her husband, who kept his word and repealed the taxes.

The tale appeared in 1188 and is first found in the *Flores Historiarum* of 1235, but the historical figures it depicts lived nearly 150 years before. Leofric was the Anglo-Saxon Earl who in 1043 built the Benedictine monastery, where Godiva was buried, that would over the years transform Coventry from a small settlement into medieval England's fourth-largest town. His wife, Godgyfu, outlived him by ten years and may have been a powerful ruler in her own right after her husband's death; she also donated money and land to the Church. The Godiva story probably evolved from a pagan fertility ritual and was popularised in the writings of the Norman chronicler Roger of Wendover during the thirteenth century. Peeping Tom was a later embellishment, dating only from the seventeenth century, inspired by the shocked face that appears at a window in a famous Renaissance painting of the scene in Coventry Museum. The face was meant to be that of Godiva's husband Leofric but the fate of Peeping Tom had already captured the public's imagination. Even Godiva's nudity may have been a fanciful elaboration. It is more likely that Leofric, if he challenged his wife at all, dared her to ride through the city without her jewellery and finery.

The longevity of the Godiva story is probably partly due to the 'Godiva Processions' introduced in the seventeenth century to open Coventry's annual summer fair and which continued until the 1800s, when the idea of young women flaunting themselves in public was frowned upon by the prudish Victorians. Today the tradition has been revived to open the Spirit of Coventry Festival each June, when a local tourist guide rides through the streets dressed in a body stocking.

Website: *Let's All Sing Together* **(www.letsallsingtogether. com)**

Let's All Sing Together is the first line of the Coventry song written by former manager and erstwhile television pundit Jimmy Hill:

> Let's all sing together, play up Sky Blues.
> While we sing together, we will never lose.
> Tottenham or Chelsea, United or anyone,
> They shan't defeat us; we'll fight till the game is won.

Crewe Alexandra

The Alexandra Athletic Club was formed in 1866 and played cricket, and probably rugby, before forming a football club called Crewe Alexandra in 1877.

The Cheshire town is close enough to the border to have a Welsh name, from *cryw* or 'creel', literally a fish basket. It acquired the sense 'stepping stones', probably because the stones were laid alongside a wickerwork fence or 'basket' placed across the small streams in Crewe to catch fish.

'Alexandra' was adopted to honour the beautiful Danish Princess Alexandra, who made an official visit to Crewe in 1876 with her husband, Queen Victoria's eldest son the Prince of Wales (the future King Edward VII), to mark the opening of the public Queen's Park named for the Prince's mother. Princess Alexandra, known as 'Alix' by her family, was Princess of Wales from 1863 to 1901 – the longest anyone has held the title – after marrying Albert Edward. As Queen from 1901 to 1910 and then Queen Mother, Alix was greatly loved by the British people. She died in 1925 at Sandringham and was buried at Windsor.

Nicknames: *Railwaymen, The Alex*
Railwaymen reflects Crewe's long history as a railway town, brought into being by the engine works of the old LNWR and the junction of the lines to Birmingham, Manchester, Liverpool and Chester. The *Alex* is an abbreviation of the club's name.

Ground: *The Alexandra Stadium, Gresty Road*
The ground, renamed after the Danish Princess Alexandra (see above) in 2000, originally took its name from the nearby road when it was opened in 1906. The majority of fans still use the traditional *Gresty Road* name rather than the *Alexandra Stadium*.

The stands are all named after their sponsors: *Air Products (Main)*, *Advance Personnel (Gresty Road)*, *BMW Bluebell (Popular Side)* and the *Charles Audi Stand*, also known as the *Railway End*, behind which is the main goods line to Chester and the north-west in a cutting a few yards beyond the boundary.

Crest
The badge was introduced in the late 1990s. It shows a red lion, like that in the town crest, taken from the arms of the Crewe family who were associated with Nantwich and other parts of the district. The family attained marquisate rank but is now extinct. The lion is also shown on the local British Railways crest holding a steam engine railway wheel, a motif once used by the club. It is set inside a laurel wreath surrounded by the words 'Crewe Alexandra Football Club', all of which is contained inside a shield.

Fanzines: *The Alex, Super Dario Land*
The Alex is the club's nickname (see **Nicknames**, above). *Super Dario Land* is named after long-serving manager Dario Gradi who has been in charge since June 1983.

Crystal Palace

A Crystal Palace club was first founded in 1861 by staff working at the Great Exhibition in Joseph Paxton's spectacular glass building. The club took part in the first FA Cup in 1871, reaching the semi-final. However, because the Crystal Palace sports ground was the venue for the Cup final, the club was rejected by the FA, which did not like the idea of the Cup final hosts running their own club. A separate company was therefore formed in 1905.

The Crystal Palace was constructed in London's Hyde Park for the Great Exhibition of 1851. It was first dubbed Crystal Palace by the satirical magazine *Punch* because of the large quantity of glass and the nickname stuck. The building, which had captured the public's imagination, was moved south to Sydenham after the exhibition and the name Crystal Palace spread to the surrounding district. It was adopted by Crystal Palace Football Club, which used the old Cup final ground at Sydenham in south London until 1915, when the army took over the site.

The sports ground was for many years one of the most prestigious homes of English football. The ground was laid out just below Paxton's glass palace in what had been an artificial lake and offered an ideal setting for fans to stroll about and enjoy picnics before and after a match. In 1895 the ground hosted the FA Cup final for the first time; another nineteen finals were staged there before the First World War, ending a year before the so-called Khaki Cup final in 1915. The Crystal Palace club moved further south to Selhurst Park in 1924 and, sadly, twelve years later the steel and glass building from which the team took its name was destroyed by fire.

Nicknames: *The Eagles, The Glaziers*
Crystal Palace used to be called *The Glaziers* because of the large amount of glass in the building after which the club is named. However, when Malcolm Allison became manager in 1973 he decided the club needed a revamp so he changed the strip to scarlet and royal blue stripes and, inexplicably, adopted the *Eagles* nickname to create a progressive image. Incidentally, Benfica and non-League Hinckley Town are also known as The Eagles.

Ground: *Selhurst Park*

After the Admiralty's takeover of the *Crystal Palace* ground at Sydenham in 1915 the club played at several venues before settling at *Selhurst Park* in 1924. The ground was named after an existing public park south of Holmesdale Road, which took its name from the local district. The stadium is situated on a former brick-field site that belonged to the London Brighton and South Coast Railway Company.

The *Arthur Wait Stand* was built in 1969 and named after the popular and successful former club chairman, who used to play football on the brick-field as a boy. Wait was a builder by trade and his firm built the stand. He was even occasionally seen working on its construction himself. The *Croydon Advertiser Family Stand (Whitehorse Lane End)* is named after the newspaper that sponsors the stand. It used to be called after the adjacent lane, which preserves the old name of an estate owned by Walter Whithors in 1367. The *Holmesdale Road Stand* is named after the nearby road.

Crest

A new crest was designed in 1973 along with the introduction of a new scarlet and blue strip and the adoption of the Eagles nickname (see **Nicknames**, above). Not surprisingly, the crest featured an eagle spreading its wings standing on a football, atop a depiction of the original Crystal Palace.

Fanzines: *Palace Echo*, *Five-Year Plan*

Palace Echo started out as *Eagle Eye (incorporating Palace Echo)* in 1987. Many people assumed *Palace Echo* had merged with *Eagle Eye* but the title was in fact a joke about the uncovered Holmesdale Road Stand, a central theme of the early issues. The title implied that one day, when there was a roof, there would be an echo. The name was changed to *Palace Echo* in 1994 under a new editor. The fanzine has had a website since January 1999 (www.palace-echo.net).

Five-Year Plan is named after former chairman Mark Goldberg's five-year plan to take Palace from the First Division into Europe. Instead, the club went into administration in the late 1990s.

Website: *The Holmesdale Online* (www.holmesdale.net)

The website is named after the Holmesdale Road Stand (see **Ground**, above).

Darlington

A football club was formed in Darlington in 1861 but the present club was founded at Darlington Grammar School in 1883.

The County Durham town has a name meaning 'settlement of Deornoth's people' with the 'n' of the personal name becoming 'l' under Norman influence. Nobody knows who Deornoth was but his name means 'animal plunder'.

Nickname: *The Quakers*

The nickname reflects the strength of the Quaker religious movement in the Darlington area since the seventeenth century. Many of the industrialists and businessmen of the eighteenth and nineteenth centuries were from strong Quaker families. Indeed, the club at one time rented their old Feethams ground from a Quaker (see **Ground**, below). The movement, officially the Religious Society of Friends, got its name from a comment by its founder George Fox (1624–91). When he appeared before the magistrates at Derby in 1650 he told Judge Bennet he should 'tremble at the name of the Lord'. The judge dismissed the organisation as a bunch of 'quakers'

Quakers broke many conventions and suffered fierce persecution. Their practical Christian way of life involved dressing simply, refusing to take oaths or remove their hats in the presence of social superiors, and abandoning all titles. They still refuse to serve as combatants in war. They have no professional ministry and are guided by the 'inner light'. The meetings for worship begin with a period of silence, which continues until a member is guided to utter a word of exhortation or teaching, of prayer or praise. The Quakers are organised in 'meetings' composed of representatives of the congregations. The Yearly Meeting carries greatest weight.

Ground: *The Williamson Motors Stadium* (formerly the *Reynolds Arena*)

Darlington moved from their old *Feethams* ground to a purpose-built stadium at Neasham Road in August 2003. The Feethams ground had been created in 1866 when the Darlington Cricket Club rented it from John Beaumont Pease, a Quaker, campaigner for the abolition of slavery and owner of Feethams House. The new 25,000 all-seater stadium on the edge of the town was named the *Reynolds Arena* after chairman George Reynolds, a local businessman who saved the club in 1999 when he paid off debts reported to be about £5 million and started construction of the club's new home. However, the costs of the Arena had left Darlington in financial difficulties again. When the club went into administration on 23 December 2003 the fans blamed Reynolds. The Sterling Consortium had loaned Reynolds a substantial sum of money to finish the ground and rather than lose their investment they took over the club. One of their first acts was to take down the name Reynolds Arena on 22 April 2004 and rename the ground the *New Stadium*. The club came out of administration at the end of the summer of 2004. The ground is now called the *Williamson Motors Stadium* after sponsorship from a local Peugeot car dealership, which began on 18 August 2004.

The stands are simply named *North*, *South East* and *West*.

Crest

The club badge shows a traditional tall black Quaker hat (see **Nickname**, above) with the nickname The Quakers at the bottom, inside a scroll, and George Stephenson's No. 1 Locomotion train. The crest had been designed by the daughter of the former owner Reg Brealey in about 1990, and was re-introduced to replace the badge used by George Reynolds, who had fallen from grace at the club (see **Ground**, above).

Darlington hit the headlines in 1825 when Stephenson's Locomotion chugged to nearby Stockton-on-Tees, with the inventor at the controls and flag-carrying horsemen riding ahead to warn of the onrushing train, which reached a speed of 10–13 mph. The line's instigator was Edward Pease, who wanted a fast and economical way to transport coal from the Durham pits to the docks of Stockton. But the novel form of transport soon proved popular with passengers and became the world's first passenger railway line after carrying its first human cargo on 27 September 1825. Subsequently, Darlington grew into a rail-engineering centre and thrived until the pruning of the network and the closure of the works in 1966. Not surprisingly, therefore, all signs in the town point to the Darlington Railway Centre and Museum in the North Road Station, which was completed in 1842. The town's North Road Railway Museum houses the original Locomotion, actually built in Newcastle, which was in service until 1841.

Website: *The Tin Shed* (www.the-tinshed.co.uk),
DAFTS (www.dafts.co.uk), *Darlo Uncovered* (http://
darlington.rivals.net)
The *Tin Shed* was a nickname for the old North Stand, a concrete
terrace with a corrugated iron roof, at the club's previous ground,
Feethams. The link to Feethams has been preserved at the New
Stadium with a bar named the Tin Shed. *DAFTS* is the acronym
for Darlington Away For Travelling Supporters, a group of exiled
and far-flung Darlington fans. *Darlo Uncovered* uses the local abbreviation of the team's name.

Derby County

The club was formed as an offshoot of the Derbyshire County Cricket Club in 1884. They had wanted to be named Derbyshire County FC, after the cricket club, but objections from the local football association, who thought the name was too long, led them to choose Derby County FC.

The county town of Derbyshire was named Deoraby, 'deer village' by the Danes who settled in the area in the ninth century. The name comes from Old Norse *djur*, 'deer', and *by*, 'village'.

Nickname: *The Rams*
The nickname is in honour of the legendary 100-foot-tall creature made famous by the eighteenth-century folksong variously entitled 'The Derby Ram' or 'The Derby Tup', which includes the lines:

> As I was going to Derby all on a market day.
> I met the finest ram, sir, that ever was fed upon hay...
> The little boys of Derby, sir, they have come to beg his eyes,
> To kick around the streets, sir, for they were football size...

The following lines were added in the 1950s:

> The s**t from the Ram, sir, it's a hundred yards around
> And it plays every Saturday upon the Baseball Ground

The nickname is also a reference to 'Private Derby', the ram kept by the local Worcestershire and Sherwood Foresters county regiment as a mascot. Their barracks was in Derby on the site of what is now a cinema. As Rick Minter explains in *Mascots – Football's Furry Friends*, 'In 1858, the 95th Derbyshire Regiment was operating in Central India during the Indian Mutiny campaign. The commanding officer noticed a fine fighting ram tethered in a yard. He directed Private Sullivan to take the ram and it followed him, marching across nearly 3,000 miles.' The ram was involved in six battles during the campaign and was honoured with the India Medal along with the rest of the regiment in 1862. Since 1912 the Duke of Devonshire has presented each new Private Derby ram from the Swaledale flock on the Chatsworth estate. Private Derby rarely visits the team on match days as they seem to lose whenever he is present.

The ram appears on the club crest and Derbyshire's coat of arms (see **Crest**, below).

Ground: *Pride Park*

From 1895 to 1997 Derby played at the *Baseball Ground,* which had been developed in the 1880s as a recreation area for foundry workers. In 1889 the foundry owner Francis Ley had visited America and was so impressed with baseball that he promoted it among his workers and spent £7,000 improving and adapting the ground for the sport. Baseball was played at the ground for some years even after Derby moved there and several clubs, such as Aston Villa, Preston and Stoke, entered teams in a summer tournament. Derby won the competition in 1897 with forward Steve Bloomer playing second base. (Home plate was in the Colombo Street corner of the pitch, behind which the terrace was known for many years as Catcher's Corner.)

At the start of the 1997–8 season Derby moved to *Pride Park.* The business park on the outskirts of the city centre of Derby, which includes Pride Park stadium, takes its name from a mixed public and private sector initiative called Derby Pride. Under this the club was offered 35 acres of a former refuse tip a mile from the Baseball Ground, between the A6 and the River Derwent, as a site on which to build a new stadium.

The stands and their sponsors are *North* (Derbyshire Building Society), *South* (Cawarden, a destruction to construction company), *West* (the Toyota car company) and *East* (ukdiggers.com, one of the Midlands' largest fleets of excavators, dumpers, etc.).

Crest

The ram is the county emblem of Derbyshire and is used as the club badge because of the club's nickname (see **Nickname**, above). Sheep were the foundation of local farming for thousands of years, and later provided raw materials for the early cloth and leather industry on which the county's towns were based.

Websites: *Ramzone* (http://derbycounty.rivals.net), *The Baseball Bat Fanzine* (www.baseballbatfanzine.co.uk)

Ramzone refers to the team nickname. *The Baseball Bat Fanzine* is named after the club's former Baseball Ground (see **Ground**, above).

Doncaster Rovers

In 1879 Albert Jenkins, a fitter at Doncaster's LNER railway works, assembled a team to play a one-off match against the Yorkshire Institution for the Deaf. The players remained together as Doncaster Rovers in response to the emerging popularity of the game in nearby Sheffield.

The Yorkshire town's name comes from the river Don and Old English *ceaster* from Latin *castra* or 'camp': Doncaster was a former Roman fort. 'Don' is a Celtic river name meaning simply 'water', 'river'. 'Rovers' indicates that the club had a series of homes in its early history.

Nickname: *Rovers*
The nickname is taken from the club name.

Ground: *The Earth Stadium, Belle Vue*
In 1922 the club moved to *Belle Vue*, which refers to the fine view of the pastures from Bawtry Road (the Great North Road). At the turn of the century the council ruled that no stands could be built at the ground, then called the Low Pastures, that would block the *belle vue*. In a move that angered some fans Belle Vue was renamed the *Earth Stadium* as part of a sponsorship deal with a Rotherham-based finance company, Earth Finance.

The stands are called *Main, Popular Terrace, Rossington End Terrace* (the *Kop*; see **Liverpool**, Ground) and *Town End*.

The council has backed a proposal for a new £20 million 15,000 capacity stadium to be shared between Rovers, Doncaster Dragons RLFC and Doncaster Belles Ladies FC. The site is next to a lake at the back of Lakeside Village a mile and a half from Belle Vue and is due to be completed in 2006.

Crest
The Viking badge was introduced in 1972 shortly after Stan Anderson became manager, because he wanted a new beginning for the club after it had been relegated to the old Fourth Division (League 2) in 1971. The new design, which was the result of a competition, replaced the old Doncaster borough crest and was

chosen because Rovers is one of several names associated with the nomadic existence of Viking warriors. The area also has links to the Scandinavian warriors (Viking remains were excavated some years later at Woodlands, a western suburb of the town). The Viking design is not connected to logos used by Rover cars, contrary to a well-known myth. The words 'Founded 1879' are displayed above the Viking warrior, who is holding a sword and a shield and wearing a cloak. A white rose, the symbol of Yorkshire, is on the shield.

Fanzines: *Popular Stand*
The fanzine takes its name from the *Popular Stand*, known for the 'pigeon box' hanging from its roof. An owl used to nest in it and fans would say that if the owl came out during a game Rovers would win.

Website: *Donny Massive* (http://doncasterrovers.rivals.net)
Donny Massive uses the local abbreviation of the team's name.

Everton

St Domingo Church Sunday School formed a football club in 1878. It played at Stanley Park, in an affluent merchants' suburb in the Liverpool district of Everton between Anfield at the top of the slope and Goodison Park at the bottom. The following year the club was attracting interest from 'folk beyond the church' and expanded its membership. At a meeting in November 1879 in the Queen's Head Hotel, Village Street, close to Ye Ancient Everton Toffee House, the club therefore changed its name to Everton, after the district west of the park in which its original headquarters was situated. Players wore black shirts with a white sash, earning the nickname the Black Watch, after the darkly dressed Highland regiment, before changing to royal blue in 1901.

The Everton district gets its name from the Old English word *Evretona*, *ton* meaning 'hill' or 'farm', although in this case it probably means that the area was on a hill overlooking the city centre. The Domesday book calls it 'Oferton', which means 'the village over and above the town'. Generally, it means a 'farmstead where wild boars are seen'.

Motto
Nil Satis, Nisi Optimum. Nothing But The Best Will Do.

Nickname: *The Toffees*
The nickname comes from Ye Ancient Everton Toffee House, which was close to the hotel where the club was founded. The original toffee lady, Old Ma Bushell, invented Everton toffees, large quantities of which were sold to supporters who came to watch the team play at Stanley Park, Priory Road and their third ground, Anfield. After the club moved to Goodison Park in 1893 sales of Everton toffees declined rapidly because of the distance to the new ground. The closest toffee shop to Goodison Park belonged to Old Mother Nobletts, who invented Everton mints to compete with her arch-rival. The new sweets, with their black and white stripes reflecting the colours of an old Everton strip, were a great success. Old Ma Bushell decided to fight back and gained permission from the club to distribute her toffees to the crowd inside the ground

before kick-off. Her beautiful young grand-daughter Jemima Bushell dressed in her best finery and donned a broad hat before carrying around her basket laden with individually wrapped toffees. Thus was born the tradition of the Everton Toffee Lady as a pre-match feature at Goodison. For years one woman performed the task (a Mrs Gorry played the role in the 1950s) but nowadays a number of different teenage girls are chosen from the ranks of the supporters club. *Toffee Web* gives a full account of the history of the club and its nickname: see **Websites**, below.

Ground: *Goodison Park*

The club played at *Stanley Park*, *Priory Road* and *Anfield*, where Everton won their first championship in 1891. They moved to *Mere Green*, a patch of wasteland described as a 'howling desert' on the north edge of Stanley Park, after they had failed to agree on a rent increase at Anfield with their wealthy landlord, a local brewer called John Houlding. The ground in the district of Walton, renamed Goodison Park because it had an entrance on Goodison Road, was the first major football stadium in England when it opened in 1892. It was nicknamed Toffeeopolis after the club's connections with Ye Ancient Everton Toffee House (see **Nickname**, above).

The *Bullens Road* and *Gwladys Street Stands* are named after nearby roads and the *Park End* after Stanley Park, the public park nearest that end of the ground, leaving the *Main Stand*.

Crest

The badge features a tower bordered by two wreaths. The tower, known as Prince Rupert's Tower or the Round House, built in 1787, is an old Bridewell or lock-up that stands on Everton Brow in Netherfield Road, Everton. Despite taking their club crest from the district of Everton the team have never played there. The club's motto (see **Motto**, above) is included in a scroll beneath the shield.

Prince Rupert's Tower first appeared on a tie in 1938 but was not officially adopted by the club until 1980. The small round house with a conical roof in the middle of a cattle enclosure was used to incarcerate wrong-doers such as drunks until they could be hauled before the magistrate the following morning. There is a display about the tower in Liverpool Museum.

The lock-up is named after Prince Rupert (1619–82), the nephew of King Charles I, who was a commander of the Royalist cavalry during the English Civil War. Rupert's mother, Elizabeth of

Bohemia, was King Charles's sister so her son gave his allegiance to Charles when the English Civil War broke out. In 1642 he was appointed to lead the Royalist cavalry where his dashing reputation earned him the nickname 'The Mad Cavalier'. He was appointed General of the Horse and after a series of military successes became General of the Royalist army in November 1644. However, defeat at Bristol in September 1645 led Charles to dismiss him from his service and he played no further part in the English Civil War. Prince Rupert's Tower is surely a misnomer, however, since he stormed Liverpool Castle during the siege of the city in 1644, while the tower was not built until 1787. The Everton programme for the game against Chelsea on 11 May 1997 states, 'Prince Rupert's Tower was one early name which referred to the fact that Prince Rupert (the Field Marshall Montgomery of his day), during the build-up to the attack on Liverpool Castle, stayed in a cottage on the top of the hill. From there, he is said to have looked down to Liverpool Castle, dismissing its importance with the words, "It's a crow's nest which any party of schoolboys could take!"'

Fanzines: *Speke From The Harbour, Satis?*
Speke From the Harbour refers to the journey taken by Irish Evertonians to Speke, the old name for Liverpool airport, from the Harbour airport in Ireland. The local district of Speke has a name meaning 'branches' or 'brushwood', like that seen floating on the Mersey. *Satis?* is taken from the club's motto (see **Motto**, above).

Websites: *Toffee Web* (www.toffeeweb.com), *When Skies Are Grey* (www.whenskiesaregrey.com), *Blue Kipper* (www.bluekipper.com)
Toffee Web comes from the club's nickname. *When Skies Are Grey* is from the terrace chant sung to the tune of 'You Are My Sunshine':

> You are my Everton, my only Everton,
> You make me happy when skies are grey,
> You never notice, how much I love you,
> So please don't take my Everton away...

Blue Kipper comes from the nickname of the fanzine editor Steve Jones.

Fulham

The club was founded by two clergymen as Fulham St Andrew's Church Sunday School FC in 1879 and nine years later adopted the name Fulham, after the district of west London beside the River Thames.

The name means 'Fulla's riverside meadow', with the personal name followed by Old English *hamm*, which means 'hemmed-in land', typically land in the bend of a river. There are no waterside meadows now but Bishop's Park, behind the Putney End of Craven Cottage, and Hurlingham Park are in a broad bend on the north bank of the Thames.

Nickname: *Cottagers*
The nickname is a reference to the cottage that forms part of the ground (see **Ground**, below).

Ground: *Craven Cottage*
The ground on the east bank of the Thames takes its name from a former hunting lodge and house built in 1780 by the sixth Baron Craven in woods that had formed part of Anne Boleyn's hunting grounds. The thatched cottage, which was later used by King George IV, soon became a local landmark and a fashionable leisure retreat for wealthy visitors, particularly after the money lender Charles King moved there in 1834. Five years later the novelist and politician Edward Bulwer-Lytton, who would become famous for his novel *The Last Days of Pompeii*, took up residence and wrote at least two of his popular historical novels, *The Last of the Barons* and *Night and Morning*, while he lived at the cottage.

Bulwer-Lytton was followed by Sir Ralph Howard, among whose guests were said to be the Prince of Wales, the Prime Minister Benjamin Disraeli and Prince Louis Napoleon. The next owner was an American, W. Bentley Woodbury, who sold up to a Surrey farmer. He rented the cottage to a retired policeman but on 8 May 1888 it burnt down and the site was left to rot until 1894, when Fulham bought the lease for the grounds. When the stadium was constructed rubble was dumped around the pitch to form low areas of banking, supplemented at the Putney End by the remains of the cottage, which stood roughly on the site of what is now the south end of the Main Stand. As the ruins were removed a labourer fell into the concealed entrance of what was claimed to be a tunnel leading under the Thames to the opposite side in Barnes.

In 1905, Fulham hired the Scottish engineer Archibald Leitch to extend Craven Cottage's three banks of terracing and erect a new stand, and a new cottage in the shape of a corner pavilion, an idea he borrowed from Scotland, where Celtic, Aberdeen and later Airdrie had such a structure. There were dressing rooms on the ground floor of the red brick cottage and an ornate, wrought iron balcony supported by columns on the first floor. A small gable on the roof was flanked by chimneys. The cottage also contained offices, a boardroom and a small flat for the use of staff or players.

The *Stevenage Road Stand* is named after the local road which commemorates a Colonel William Stevenage who died in Fulham in 1709. The *Hammersmith End* is named after the nearby district. The *Riverside Stand* (formerly the Eric Miller Stand) was opened in February 1972 and named after the River Thames, which runs alongside. Eric Miller was a Fulham director who had used his contacts to get the stand built. He committed suicide in the midst of a financial and political scandal in 1977. He was not liked by the fans, partly because the decision to build the stand at a time of high inflation got the club into financial difficulties in a period when their gates had halved since they were relegated from the top flight in 1968. The *Putney End* is also named after the nearby district.

Crest

The current crest, introduced in May 2001, is the fourth completely new design. The letters FFC, popular during the mid-1970s, are linked together in the team's reserve colour of red, with the main black and white colours represented by the crest's wide bars. The crest was created after the club found that only 14 per cent of fans recognised the old crest, and also to give Fulham control over its identity since the previous crest, owned by the London Borough of Hammersmith and Fulham, presented trademark problems. The crest's modern outline shape is the same as the old one but the clean and distinctive bold outline emphasises stability.

Websites: *Unofficial Cottagers* (www.fulham-mad.co.uk/
index.asp), *Back To The Cottage* (www.backtothecottage.
co.uk), *There's Only One F in Fulham* (http://fulham.rivals.
net/default.asp?sid=906), *The Green Pole* (www.thegreenpole.
pwp.blueyonder.co.uk)

Unofficial Cottagers and *Back To The Cottage* refer to the club nickname, the Cottagers, from their Craven Cottage stadium (see
Ground, above). The Fulham Supporters' Trust began as the 'Back
to the Cottage' campaign, formed after the club announced it had
ditched plans to redevelop Craven Cottage on the lines of the planning permission received in February 2001. What began as a small
group of like-minded fans soon developed into an umbrella organisation supported by the independent Fulham Supporters' Club.
Following a well attended public meeting at Hammersmith Town
Hall, fans decided to establish a Supporters' Trust.

One F in Fulham takes its name from the title of the common football song adapted by various clubs to their own team names and
widely heard at grounds around the country. *The Green Pole* is named
after the 'green pole' that supports the roof at the Hammersmith
End of Craven Cottage. The pole is directly behind the goal at the
'home' end and the more vocal Fulham supporters congregate
around it. When the ground was refurbished, the club added an
extension to the existing roof, supported by two new grey poles.
Many fans asked the club if the 'green pole' was staying, as it was
very important to them. Strangely enough, it remains, and is still
green. The club either ran out of grey paint or maybe bowed to the
fans' pressure.

Gillingham

The club was founded as Excelsior in 1893 in the wake of the success of another local club, the Royal Engineers of Chatham, made up of a team of officers. At a meeting in the Napier Arms, Brompton, later that year Excelsior became New Brompton, a suburb of the borough of Gillingham, before changing its name to Gillingham in 1913.

Gillingham, one of the Medway towns in Kent, means 'the homestead of the family or followers of a man called Gylla'.

Nickname: *The Gills*
The nickname is a reference to the club name.

Ground: *Priestfield Stadium*
When the club became New Brompton it purchased a piece of land owned by the church near Gillingham Road. Originally called the *New Brompton Athletic Ground*, it became known as *Priestfield Road* after the road behind the Gillingham End, so named because of the area's connection with the church. The club adopted the grander name *Priestfield Stadium* in 1947.

The *Main Medway Stand* is named after the local area. The *Brian Moore Stand* (formerly the *Gillingham End* or *Town End Terrace*) is named after the late Gillingham director and popular commentator Brian Moore (see **Fanzines**, below). The balding, round-faced, toothy Moore was ITV's principal football reporter for thirty years. He covered nine World Cups and more than twenty Cup finals, becoming known as the 'Voice of Football'. However, in his opinion the highlight of his career was covering England's World Cup triumph over West Germany in 1966 as a young BBC radio commentator. He prepared meticulously for every match and his uncomplicated, economical style appealed to the viewers. One critic described the calm and composed Moore as sounding like a 'spectator at ease'.

Born on 28 February 1932 to farm labourers who hailed from Benenden in Kent, Moore went on to win a scholarship to Cranbrook public school, where he became head boy and captain of the hockey and cricket teams. He also developed an affection for his local football club, Gillingham. After national service with the RAF he took up his first job in 1954 as a sub-editor on the monthly *World Sports* magazine, at the time one of the most respected publications in its field and endorsed by the British Olympic Association. In 1956 he joined the Exchange Telegraph (ExTel) news agency, which subjected him to the hard discipline of endless match reports, often in uncomfortable conditions under strict time pressure.

In 1958 Moore joined *The Times*, where style was more of a priority, and three years later he joined BBC Radio as a sports commentator. Sports television was keen to recruit talent from radio and in 1968 Moore received a call from Jimmy Hill asking him to join London Weekend Television, where he established himself as the key commentator on the station's flagship Sunday football programme *The Big Match*. He also worked for ITV's *Midweek Sports Special* from 1978 until 1986. His one big gaffe occurred after Nottingham Forest won the European Cup in 1980 in Madrid. He ended the programme by announcing to an audience of 15 million: 'So Hamburg win the European Cup.' However, his mistakes were very rare.

In his obituary in the *Guardian* Brian Glanville wrote: 'He remained modest, affable and unaffected [by the massive television exposure], well liked not only by his colleagues in the media but by football players themselves. Perhaps this had something to do with the fact that he was a fan at heart.' Moore retired after the 1998 World Cup in France and underwent heart surgery for the second time in 1995, although he continued to work, saying defiantly that he was 'aiming to reach 90'. His final television assignment was a series of twenty interviews with players of the past for Sky Television in 1999. Moore died aged 69 on 1 September 2001.

The *Rainham End Stand* is named after Rainham, the neighbouring town to Gillingham. The *Gordon Road Stand* is named after the nearby road.

Crest

The current badge was designed in 1993 to mark Gillingham's centenary. It shows Invicta, a white rampant horse, on the right half and black and white stripes on the left. Invicta is the symbol of the county of Kent dating from 1066, when William the Conqueror was crowned King of England. At that time Kent was still unconquered by the Norman invaders, as symbolised by Invicta, the untamed horse. Gillingham played in black and white striped shirts from 1893, when they were known as New Brompton FC, until they changed their colours to royal blue for the 1931–2 season. The Latin phrase on the crest, *Domus Clamantium*, means 'Home of the Shouting Men' and refers to the ancient tribe who came from Gillingas, an area referred to in the Domesday Book as Gellingeham.

Fanzine: *Brian Moore's Head Looks Uncannily Like London Planetarium*
'Brian Moore's Head' is the title of a song by the quirky, football-obsessed, post-punk band Half Man Half Biscuit, which refers to the shape of the late Gillingham director's famous bald head. It was a joke which, characteristically, Moore (see **Ground**, above) gladly shared.

Websites: *Gills Connect* (http://gillingham.rivals.co.uk.net), *Gills 365* (http://www.gillingham-mad.co.uk)
Gills Connect and *Gills 365* both refer to the club's nickname (see **Nickname**, above).

Grimsby Town

Grimsby Pelham FC was formed at a meeting held at the Wellington Arms in September 1878. Pelham is the name of the Earls of Yarborough, who are big landowners in the area. After a year the club changed its name to Grimsby Town, even though it has always played in nearby Cleethorpes except for a ten-year residence in Grimsby from 1889 (see **Ground**, below).

The port at the mouth of the River Humber in Lincolnshire has a Scandinavian name meaning 'Grim's village'. *Grim*, meaning 'a masked person who looks grim', was one of the names of the Scandinavian god Odin, and the Danes who named Grimsby may have had him in mind; the ending *-by* is Old Norse for 'village' and is often found in place names in this part of England.

Nickname: *The Mariners*

The nickname is a reference to the town's long maritime tradition. Grimsby has been a fishing and trading port since the eleventh century. It remains the chief fishing port in England, although the size of the catch has greatly declined in recent years. The Grimsby docks and the many warehouses of the frozen food companies, which make Grimsby 'Europe's Food Town', are behind the Pontoon End (see **Ground**, below).

Ground: *Blundell Park*

Blundell Park was close to the club's first ground at Clee Park and formed part of the land that Lord Torrington described in 1791 as 'three miles of boggy turf' on the coastal approach to Grimsby from the south. The land had been part of the manor of Itterby, purchased by Sidney Sussex college, Cambridge in 1616 with money left to it by Peter Blundell, a very wealthy merchant of Tiverton and London who died unmarried in April 1601. In 1899 Grimsby developed the land on the site of a former brickworks a few hundred yards from the sea. Blundell Park is not in Grimsby but in the nearby holiday resort of Cleethorpes, although since the two authorities merged in 1996 it now lies within the borough of Grimsby and Cleethorpes.

The *Osmond Stand*, at the Cleethorpes end, was named after one of a family of benefactors. The *John Smith's Stand* is named after the brewers who sponsor the stand. It was formerly called the *Barrett Stand*, after alderman Frank Barrett, a patron of the club, then renamed the *Findus Stand* because the new stand, opened in August 1982, was partly financed by the frozen fish company, who contributed £200,000 towards the £425,000 cost. It was later known as the *Stones Bitter Stand*, after the brewers who were sponsors, but is now known as *The Smith's Stand*, comprising the Upper Smith's and Lower Smith's. The *Pontoon Stand* refers to the Alexandra Dock, named after Princess Alexandra (see **Crewe Alexandra**), which had only recently been opened when the stand was built for the 1899–1900 season, and the strong fishing heritage of the town. The pontoon was where the fish was sold after it had been landed and was therefore the centre of the fishing industry. People came off the docks on a Saturday morning, went to the pubs and then to the match.

Crest
The Mariners still carry the fishing traditions of the town on their crest, which was designed in the mid-1950s. The badge shows a trawler and three fish (thought to be linked to England's Three Lions), inside a shield of black and white stripes.

Fanzine: *Sing When We're Fishing*
The fanzine is named after the terrace chant 'Sing When You're Fishing', sung by opposing fans to the refrain of the song 'Guantanamera', which was first heard on the Kop at Anfield in 1979 during a 5–0 hammering by Liverpool. The original lyrics of 'La Guantanamera' consisted of the opening stanzas of a poem, 'Versos Sencillos', or 'Simple Verses' by Jose Martí. Martí was a Cuban hero, a writer and intellectual who died in 1895 fighting for Cuba's independence from Spain. The song as we know it today was written by Julián Orbón, who combined Joseito Fernandez Diaz's original music with Martí's lyrics. Both Díaz's and Orbón's 'Guantanamera' versions share a famous chorus: 'Guantanamera, guajira guantanamera, Guantanamera, guajira guantanamera.' Martí's immensely popular verses were combined with the chorus so as to suggest that the song is addressed to a young woman from Guantanamo on the southern tip of the island.

Websites: *Jailhouse Rock* (http://home.world-online.no/ grimsby), *Cod Almighty* (www.codalmighty.com), *Three Fish* (www.three-fish.co.uk), *Electronic Fishcake* (http:// grimsbytown.rivals.net)

All the website names refer to the club's fishing connections. *Jailhouse Rock* is taken from the Elvis Presley classic; *Cod Almighty* reflects the fans' many frustrations at their team's performances, echoing the common exclamation. *Three Fish* refers to the number of fish on the club crest (see **Crest**, above). *Electronic Fishcake* was originally the Grimsby Town International Suppporters' Club website. It gradually developed into a site for all Mariners fans. It is known as *The Fishy*.

Hartlepool United

A club called Hartlepools United was formed in 1908 on the back of the success of a West Hartlepool club that had existed since 1881, and had won the FA Amateur Cup in 1905 before folding in 1910. The club dropped the 's' in 1968 when it became plain Hartlepool, before restoring United in 1977.

The name of the town and port near Middlesbrough relates to the bay, meaning 'hart island pool': 'Hart Island', or simply 'Hart', was the original name of the pool or bay near the peninsula on which the town stands today. The reference is probably to the harts (male deer) that lived on the headland, rather than to its shape. The middle 'le' represents the original word for island.

Nickname: *The Pool*
Pool is taken from the club name. (See also *Monkey Hangers*, under **Fanzine**, below).

Ground: *Victoria Park*
In 1908 the club took over the *Victoria Ground*, a former rubbish tip opposite the Hartlepool docks that had been the home of West Hartlepool rugby club since 1886. It was named after Queen Victoria in honour of her Golden Jubilee the following year. The club changed the name of the ground to *Victoria Park* in the 1990s.

The *Cyril Knowles (Main) Stand* was named after the club's former manager, the Tottenham Hotspur full back remembered for the song 'Nice One Cyril'. He was in charge at United from 1989 until he died of a brain tumour in 1991, aged just 47. However, he will be best remembered for a playing career in which he won the UEFA Cup (1972), the FA Cup (1967) and two League Cups (1971 and 1973). He played 504 games for Spurs, scoring 17 goals after joining the north London club in 1964 for £45,000 as a virtual unknown, from Middlesbrough. The *Camerons (Mill House) Stand* is named after the local Camerons brewery, which has been a prominent sponsor and advertiser with the club for years. The Mill House is a nearby pub. The *Expamet Town End* is the end nearest the town, which is just a few hundred yards away. Expamet (Expanded Metal Company) is a long-established business, known locally as the

Expansion, which makes the metal mesh of its name, along with barrier fences and street furniture. The *Rink End Stand* is named after the popular Queen's ice skating rink, which later became a ballroom. It stood behind the stand but was demolished in the 1970s.

Crest

The badge shows a ship's wheel, reflecting the town's heritage as a port and shipbuilding centre. 'Hartlepool United FC' appears at the top of the crest, a football in the centre and the inscription 'The town's club' on a scroll at the bottom.

Fanzine: *Monkey Business*

Monkey Business is so-called because Hartlepool supporters are known locally as the Monkey Hoyers (hangers). This dates back to a legend from the time of the Napoleonic Wars with France (1793–1815) when a French ship was wrecked off the coast of Hartlepool. At the time there was fear of a French invasion of Britain and much public concern about the possibility of French infiltrators and spies. There were no survivors from the wreck except the mascot, a monkey dressed in a military uniform, which managed to get safely to land. It was captured by some local fishermen, who tried to speak to it and ask it questions. They could not understand its replies and, having never seen a monkey before, thought it was a strangely shaped person speaking in a foreign language. The townspeople, who were not widely travelled, decided it was speaking French and was therefore a spy. It was condemned to death and hanged on the Fish Sands in front of the Town Wall. *Monkey Business*, which also has a website (www.bizz.hufc.net), is named after the travails of the poor monkey. The club's mascot is a monkey called H'Angus, which is 'Hang Me' in Hartlepool dialect.

However, there is no evidence of any truth in the legend, nor that it is very old. The first mention of the monkey is in the mid-nineteenth century, when Ned Corvan, a famous Geordie comic and singer-songwriter, first performed the 'Monkey Song' at the Dock Hotel Music Hall, Southgate, in old Hartlepool Borough. He was influenced in his act by Billy Purvis, another Geordie comic, who was very popular in Hartlepool earlier in the century. Corvan composed a song about Purvis, who had died in Hartlepool. It was very well received and Corvan soon became very popular in Hartlepool himself and played there regularly. He toured from North Yorkshire to the Scottish lowlands and about this time may have come into contact with the song 'And the Boddamers hung the Monkey O', about the villagers of the seaside village of Boddam near Peterhead in Scotland who hanged a monkey because it was the only survivor from a local shipwreck – the salvage rights could only be claimed if there were no survivors. There is a great similarity between the choruses of the two songs.

The popularity of the legend may be the result of the rivalry between West Hartlepool and old Hartlepool in the 1850s. The towns of Hartlepool and West Hartlepool had come into being as a direct result of an increased demand for coal which led to the creation of their docks and railways. There was thus a great rivalry between the rail and shipping companies. The bad feeling between the neighbouring towns dragged on for years. In the 1850s, when tempers were running very high, a song portraying the old fishermen of Hartlepool as a little less than intelligent or admirable became popular in the new West Hartlepool. (In Hartlepool Museum's Robert Wood collection of ephemera there is a poster that mentions 'aquatic monkeys' but the now obscure jibe seems to be aimed at the supporters of the West Dock, which became West Hartlepool.) This theory is also not completely watertight, however. Corvan's first performance of the song was in 'old' Hartlepool Borough and it may be that the song only became popular when the 'West Dockers' of West Hartlepool adopted it and used it against the inhabitants of old Hartlepool.

Regardless of the source of the story, the legend was spread by the most important rugby team of the old Borough, Hartlepool Rovers. In the 1890s they took a stuffed monkey with them on tour and hung it on a crossbar before a match. The team, whose home ground was the first venue for a Barbarians match, were very successful during this period. They still use a hanging monkey as their emblem. Hartlepool Yacht Club has also had a stuffed monkey as a mascot for many years. The words of the song are available today on a postcard sold locally.

Websites: *Hangems* (**www.hangems.co.uk**), *Pools Online* (**www.sportnetwork.net/main/584.php**)
Hangems is named after the story of the French monkey (see **Fanzine**, above). *Pools Online* is a reference to the team nickname.

Huddersfield Town

The club was founded in September 1908 by the Huddersfield Association Football Ground Company after a meeting at the Albert Hotel.

The name of the Yorkshire town means 'Hudraed's open land' with the rare Anglo Saxon personal name followed by Old English *feld*, 'open land' or 'field'. Another theory is that the first part of the name comes from the Old English word *huder* or 'shelter'.

Nickname: *The Terriers*

In 1970 the club's commercial director Bill Brook decided the team needed a nickname and came up with the idea of the Yorkshire terrier, a dog known for its persistence and courage (see **Crest**, below).

Ground: *The Galpharm Stadium*

The construction and engineering firm Alfred McAlpine built the stadium, which opened in 1994, and were its original sponsors. The company did not renew its sponsorship, and the ground has since taken the name of the pharmaceutical firm Galpharm. However, Robert Pepper of the Supporters Trust says: 'McAlpine is the name we had when we started here ten years ago and so many still call it that. Some fans still call the ground Leeds Road, even though that's the name of the old stadium before we moved here.'

The *Lawrence Batley (Riverside) Stand* is named after the late Lawrence Batley, a successful local businessman and Town fan who also donated money to the town's main theatre; this too is named in his honour. The River Colne that runs behind the stand explains the *Riverside* name. *John Smith's Kilner Bank Stand* is named after the brewery that sponsors the stand and the tree-covered banking that rises up behind the stadium. The *Travelworld South Stand* is named after the local sponsors, a company that was owned by former Town chairman Terry Fisher. The *Panasonic North Stand* is named after the Japanese consumer electronics company that sponsors the stand.

Crest

In 1970 the club's commercial director Bill Brook decided the crest needed to be spruced up to reflect the team's nickname (see above). A Yorkshire terrier with his paw on a football atop a mass of foliage was therefore added to the existing badge, while two castles and three sheep disappeared. A dog called Skippy belonging to a supporter, Beryl Fisher, was used as the model for the crest and became the club's first terrier mascot. He was described as 'an appealing dog with all the grit and determination in the world'. The original badge, which had been used since 1919, represented the area and was based on the Ramsden crest, since the family owned most of Huddersfield at the time. Two white roses represent Yorkshire pride, while Huddersfield castle is represented by a turret. The castle, which towers over the stadium and can be seen from almost any point in the town, was one of the few pieces of land not owned by the Ramsdens at the start of the century.

Fanzine: *Those Were The Days*
Those Were The Days refers to the 1920s when Huddersfield won the First Division (Premier League) championship three times in a row (1924–6), were runners-up twice (1927–8) and also lifted the FA Cup (1922) as well as being runners-up in that competition twice (1920 and 1928). The following decade they were once more FA Cup runners-up twice (1930 and 1938) and First Division championship runners-up (1934).

Websites: *Down at the Mac* (www.downatthemac.com), *Terrier Bytes* (www.terrier-bytes.com)
Down at the Mac refers to the ground's former name, the McAlpine Stadium. *Terrier Bytes* is a reference to the club's nickname.

Hull City

The club was formed in 1904 in an area dominated by Rugby League. It folded in 1943 and re-formed the following year. The club is named after the port city of Kingston-upon-Hull, which lies where the River Hull joins the much larger River Humber.

The city itself takes its name from the river whose name is probably very old and may come from a Celtic root word for 'muddy' or an Old Scandinavian word meaning 'deep'.

Nickname: *The Tigers*
The nickname is a reference to the team's black and amber striped shirts. It was first used by the *Hull Daily Mail* newspaper.

Ground: *Kingston Communications (KC) Stadium*
The *KC Stadium*, as it is commonly known, was opened in December 2002 after the club moved from *Boothferry Park* where they had settled in 1946. It is named after the stadium's sponsor, a telecommunications provider formed in 1999 and based in Kingston-upon-Hull, mainly serving the East Yorkshire area.

The stands are all named and sponsored as follows: the *De Vries West Stand* (a Honda car dealers), the *Ideal Standard East Stand* (a bathroom products manufacturer), the *MKM South Stand* (a building supplies company) and the *Smith & Nephew North Stand* (a medical equipment company).

Crest
The current tiger crest was introduced in 2001 after Adam Pearson bought the club and replaced the unpopular design from the previous regime. It features the tiger image first used in the 1970s. The Tigers is the club's nickname (see **Nickname**, above).

Fanzines: *Amber Nectar, The Three O'Clock at Kempton, We Are Hull, City Independent, Last Train to Boothferry Halt*
Amber Nectar (www.ambernectar.com) takes its name from the club's amber shirts. *The Three O'Clock at Kempton* is explained by the fact that the Kempton was the fans' nickname for the East Stand,

which had the best atmosphere at Hull's old Boothferry Park ground. 'Three o'clock' refers to the time when matches kicked off before fixture schedules were changed to suit television and the police. Shamelessly nostalgic. Of course, Kempton is also a well-known race course so to non-Hull City fans *The Three O'Clock At Kempton* (www.thekempton.com) looks as though it's John McCririck's domain rather than John Motson's. Moreover, the Kempton Stand used to have a station for fans, so the fanzine title could suggest a train departure time. It is one of those fanzine names that is deliberately intended only to be understood by supporters of that club. *Last Train to Boothferry Halt* takes its name from the club's Boothferry Halt station at their old Boothferry Park Ground (see **Ground**, above).

Website: *On Cloud Seven* (www.oncloudseven.com)
On Cloud Seven is a quote from an interview with the former Hull manager Colin Appleton (1982–4) on Radio Humberside in May 1989, on his return to the club. Asked how he felt to be back, Appleton replied that he was 'on cloud seven'. Appleton was ironically referring to the famous expression 'on cloud nine' but the expression 'on cloud seven', although two notches lower, does also mean 'in a euphoric state'. Indeed, both forms have co-existed since the 1950s. The saying is originally American and taken from terminology used by the United States Weather Bureau to categorise clouds. Cloud nine is cumulo-nimbus, a cumulus cloud of great vertical extent that may reach 30–40,000 feet. 'Cloud nine' seems to have become an expression for something more memorable than cloud seven because of the popularity of the *Johnny Dollar* radio show in the 1950s. In one recurring episode the hero was repeatedly knocked unconscious and transported to cloud nine.

Ipswich Town

The club was formed at a meeting in the Town Hall in 1878 when a Mr T.C. Cobbold MP, was voted president (see **Fanzines**, below). Originally it was called the Ipswich Association Football Club (AFC) to distinguish it from the older Ipswich FC, which played rugby. The two clubs amalgamated in 1888 and rugby was dropped in 1893.

The Suffolk town and port on the River Orwell was named Gipeswic by the Anglo-Saxons. The name comes from the River Gipping, a tributary of the much larger Orwell, which takes its name from the village near Newmarket whose own name means 'harbour or trading place of Gip's people'. Ipswich is therefore the personal name 'Gip' followed by Old English *wic*, meaning 'port' or 'landing place'.

Nicknames: *Blues, Town*

Blues comes from the team's colours; *Town* is a reference to the club's name.

Ground: *Portman Road*

The ground is situated on *Portman Road*, which got its own name from the word used for an alderman in the days when Ipswich was a thriving port. (An alderman is a co-opted member of an English county or borough council, next in dignity to the mayor.) The whole area where the stadium now stands was once bleak marshland traditionally granted as grazing land to the town's Portmen. The ground, which was Corporation-owned and had been used for football and other sports events for some years, was first played on by Ipswich in 1884 and acquired by the club in 1888.

The *Cobbold (East) Stand* was named after the Cobbold family, who have been connected with the club since its formation in 1878 (see above and **Fanzine**, below). Its former name was the *Portman Stand*. The *West (Britannia) Stand* is named after the sponsors, the Britannia Building Society. The *South (Greene King) Stand* is named after the local brewery based in Bury St Edmunds, which sponsors the stand. It was formerly the *Churchman's Stand* after the Churchman brothers, one of whom played in goal for Ipswich during the late 1880s. The brothers owned a tobacco processing plant behind that end of the ground where Players manufactured cigars. The factory made way for an office supplies superstore.

The road around the stadium, *Sir Alf Ramsey Way*, is named after the club's former manager who led Ipswich from the Third Division South when he took over in 1955 to the First Division (now Premier League) title in 1962, the year after the club won the Second Division (now Championship). However, his greatest triumph was taking England to World Cup success in 1966 at Wembley when they beat West Germany 4–2 after extra time. Ramsey was born on 22 January 1920 in Dagenham, Essex. He played for Southampton from 1943–9 before joining Tottenham Hotspur. He won a League Championship winner's medal in 1951, after he had helped Tottenham to the Second Division title the previous year, a double feat he later achieved as manager of Ipswich. He played more than 250 League and cup games for Spurs at right back and went on to captain England three times. His calmness and tactical awareness earned him the nickname the General. Ramsey retired from playing in 1955 to become Ipswich manager before taking the England job in 1963. He was sacked from this in 1974 after England failed to qualify for the World Cup finals. Ramsey died on 28 April 1999.

Crest

The current badge, which was given a slight facelift in 1995, shows a white Suffolk Punch horse on a shield with the turrets of the Wolsey Gate at the top and waves at the bottom, representing the sea. The club name is shown just below the turrets. The badge was designed by John Gammage, a former postmaster and treasurer of the Supporters' Club, and was the winning entry in a club competition. Gammage died during the 1993–4 season.

Gammage is quoted on the club's official website (www.itfc.co.uk) as saying that he 'regarded the Suffolk Punch as a noble animal, well suited to dominate our design and represent the club and to complete the badge I thought of the town of Ipswich'.

The Wolsey Gate, next to the fourteenth-century St Peter's Church, is all that remains of Cardinal College, named after Cardinal Thomas Wolsey (1475–1530), the son of a butcher and a native of Ipswich. In 1515 he was created a cardinal and became Lord Chancellor of England. During the next ten years he was one of the most powerful men in Europe. Under him the smaller English monasteries were dissolved and his enthusiasm for the New Learning was reflected in Cardinal College (later Christ Church) at Oxford and the college in Ipswich that he established in 1527. Shakespeare wrote in his play *Henry VIII* of 'those twins of learning, Ipswich and Oxford'. College Street in Ipswich is named after the college. Wolsey's reluctance to help Henry VIII divorce Catherine of Aragon led to his downfall in 1529. The following year he was charged with high treason and arrested.

Fanzine: *A Load of Cobbolds*

A *Load of Cobbolds* is a play on the expression 'a load of cobblers' and is derived from the surname of the club's first president, Mr T.C. Cobbold (see **Ground**, above), whose family owned the Tolly Cobbold brewery. There have been various Cobbolds on the board over the years. Philip Hope-Cobbold is a current director of the club. 'Cobblers' is rhyming slang meaning 'nonsense': cobblers' awls – balls. An awl is a shoemaker's tool.

Websites: *Pride of Anglia* (www.prideofanglia.com), *Those Were The Days* (www.twtd.co.uk), *Singing the Blues* (www.sportnetwork.net/main/s78.htm)

Pride of Anglia refers to the region in which Ipswich is based, East Anglia, and also taunts the club's local rivals Norwich City. *Those Were The Days* harks back to the successful period under manager Bobby Robson, who was in charge from January 1969 to July 1982. During this time Ipswich won the FA Cup (1978) the UEFA Cup (1981) and were runners-up in the First Division (now Premier League) twice (1981 and 1982). Robson, nicknamed 'the King of East Anglia', left the club for an eight-year reign as England manager which culminated in England's World Cup semi-final defeat in a penalty shootout by Germany in 1990. He was later knighted for services to football. *Singing the Blues* is the title of the supporters' song, based on the original written by Melvin Endsley and sung by Guy Mitchell:

> I've never felt more like singing the Blues,
> When Ipswich win and Norwich lose,
> Oh Ipswich, you've got me singing the Blues!

Leeds United

In 1904 Leeds City football club was founded by members of Hunslet AFC. Leeds City was expelled from the Football League and wound up by the Football Association in October 1919 after allegations of illegal payments to players and the club's refusal to allow the League access to its books. A month later, Leeds United was formed.

Leeds has a Celtic name, originally that of the region, meaning 'people living by the strongly flowing river', in this case the River Aire.

Nickname: *Peacocks*

Peacocks comes from the Old Peacock pub opposite the stadium, which gave its name to the sports ground run by Bentley's brewery on the Elland Road site from 1882. The pub, which has been rebuilt, is opposite the South Stand (see **Ground**, below).

Ground: *Elland Road*

The ground is named after the town of Elland, to the west of Leeds near Huddersfield. 'Elland' means 'cultivated land, or estate, by the river'. It originally belonged to Leeds Rugby Club and later Holbeck Rugby Club but was acquired by Leeds City in 1904.

The stands are called *South, East* and *West (Main)*. The *Revie (North) Stand* is named after the former manager Don Revie. A plaque in the lower concourse states that the stand was re-opened and officially renamed by the Earl of Harewood in the presence of Revie's widow Elsie on 16 October 1994. Revie became player-manager at Leeds in March 1961, having joined from Sunderland in 1958. The club just escaped relegation from the Second Division (now the Championship) in his first full season in charge but by the early 1970s the man nicknamed 'the Godfather' had transformed Leeds into one of Europe's strongest clubs. Leeds won their first First Division (now Premier League) title in 1969 and another in 1974, their only FA Cup in 1972, the League Cup in 1968 and the Fairs Cup in 1968 and 1971. Revie left Elland Road to become the England manager in 1974. In 1988 he revealed he was suffering from motor neurone disease; he died in May 1989.

Crest

The badge includes the cursive 'LUFC' as a reminder of the logo that Revie's team first wore on their shirts in the 1972 FA Cup-winning season. The logo replaced the lone owl badge, ditched by the superstitious manager, who believed birds were unlucky. On either side of LUFC are some fancy chevrons in blue and gold, above sits a football in a Yorkshire rose, included to show pride in the county and the city.

Fanzines: *To Ell And Back, The Hanging Sheep, Till The World Stops, Marching on Together*

To Ell And Back (www.toellandback.com) is a play on the name of the ground, Elland Road, and pre-dates the club's rise and fall under its chairman Peter Ridsdale. *The Hanging Sheep* is taken from the Leeds City crest, which shows a sheep in a harness being weighed as a symbol of the town's staple trade. *Till The World Stops* is taken from a line in the song officially called 'Leeds Leeds Leeds' but more commonly known as 'Marching on Together'. The song started out as the B-side of the single *Leeds United*, which reached number 10 in the charts in May 1972. *Marching on Together* also took its name from the song and was published as 'Marchin' on Together' by the Leeds fans' anti-racist campaign:

> Here we go with Leeds United, we're gonna give the boys a
> > hand
> Stand up and sing for Leeds United, they are the greatest in
> > the land...
> We love you Leeds! Leeds! Leeds!
> Marchin' on together, we're gonna see you win
> We're so proud, we shout it out loud,
> We love you Leeds! Leeds! Leeds!

Leicester City

A group of young players, mostly Wyggeston School old boys, formed Leicester Fosse FC in 1884 at a meeting in a house on the Roman Fosse Way (the Roman military road between Lincoln and Cirencester, which takes its name from the ditch, or fosse, on either side). Financial problems after the First World War led to Leicester Fosse being wound up in 1919. The old borough of Leicester had been granted city status that summer, and the club was therefore re-formed as Leicester City.

The first part of the name of the Midlands city probably comes from the small stream called the Leire, a tributary of the River Soar, which became associated with the people who lived there. The second part of the name comes from Old English *ceaster* meaning 'a Roman camp'. 'Leicester' therefore means 'Roman camp at the place of the people who lived by the Leire'.

Nickname: *Foxes*
The nickname is a reference to Leicestershire's fox-hunting tradition. The county is home to the Quorn, one of the oldest foxhunts in the country.

Ground: *Walkers Stadium*
The club moved into the new *Walkers Stadium* from *Filbert Street* at the start of the 2002–3 season. The 32,500 seater stadium was built on the site of a former power station on the banks of the River Soar, at a cost of £37 million.

The ground takes its name from the sponsors, Walkers, a snack food manufacturer best known for crisps. Walkers is named after Henry Walker, who moved from Mansfield to Leicester in the 1880s to take over a high street butcher's shop. Meat rationing after the Second World War led the company to look at alternatives and it began hand-slicing and frying potatoes to make crisps, which were already becoming increasingly popular. The road that runs around the stadium is called *Filbert Way*, named after the club's old stadium. Fans who object to sponsored stadiums still call the ground Filbert Street.

The *East (Alliance & Leicester) Stand* is named after the local building society. The *Lineker (North) Stand* is named after the former striker Gary Lineker, now a BBC sports presenter, who began his career at Leicester in 1977 and three years later helped the team win the Second Division (now Championship) title. He was called up by England for the first time in 1984 and left for Everton a year later after scoring 95 goals for Leicester in 194 League games. In 1986 he won two Player of the Year awards after scoring thirty League goals, and was top scorer at the World Cup with six goals. Lineker moved to Barcelona in July of that year, winning Spanish Cup and European Cup Winners' Cup medals before joining Tottenham Hotspur in 1989. He scored four goals in England's run to the World Cup semi-finals in 1990 and lifted the FA Cup with Spurs in 1991. Lineker retired with eighty caps, having scored forty-eight goals, one behind Bobby Charlton's record. He was awarded the OBE in 1992 and was included in the Football League Centenary 100 players. The name *Fosse Kop (South Stand)* is taken from the club's original name, Leicester Fosse (see also **Liverpool**, Ground). The name was the winning entry in a competition. Mark Bassett, the winner, said 'I wanted to connect our proud history with our bright future.'

Crest

The latest club crest, showing the head of a fox on a circular badge (see **Nickname**, above), was introduced for the 1992–3 season. It was designed by Chris Lymn, who says:

> We researched the existing and past club badges carefully and noticed there was no 'city' connection, which we found strange, so we decided to combine a city and county presence and retained the fox. We were aware that the previous foxes were portrayed in a running mode, which we felt was unfortunate as foxes only run away and never win. So we designed a head-on fox to give it some attitude. We also wanted to avoid a political stance and dropped previous references to hunting.

The fox is shown on a background of a cinqfoil of ermine, taken from the arms of the Beaumont family. Robert de Beaumont became the first Earl of Leicester in 1103. The cinqfoil, a plant with compound leaves of five leaflets, also forms part of the centrepiece of Leicester city council's coat of arms. The fur of the ermine, a carnivorous animal of the weasel family, is used in the robes of judges and is an emblem of honour and purity.

Fanzines: *The Fosse, O'Neill and Pray, When You're Smiling*
The Fosse takes its name from the Roman road where the club was
formed (see above). *O'Neill and Pray* refers to the club's former
manager Martin O'Neill. Under O'Neill Leicester enjoyed consid-
erable success between 1995 and 2000: the club won the League
Cup twice (1997 and 2000) and were runners-up in 1999. 'When
You're Smiling', sung by City fans, is thought to have been adopted
in the late 1970s because it was on the jukebox in the pub near to
where the buses to away games departed.

Websites: *For Fox Sake* (www.forfoxsake.com), *The Fox
Fanzine* (www.foxfanzine.com), *The Cunning Fox*
(www.norfox.net), *Foxes Mad* (www.leicestercity-mad.
co.uk)
For Fox Sake is wordplay linking the common terrace curse with the
club's nickname. *The Cunning Fox* and *Foxes Mad*, which is also a
printed fanzine, similarly refer to the nickname.

Leyton Orient

There is some doubt about the club's origins and its early history has become confused with teams such as Leyton and Clapton. However, it is most likely that Leyton Orient was formed originally by members of Homerton Theological College who established Glyn Cricket Club in 1881 and continued playing football through the following winter. The cricket club became the Eagle Cricket Club. The football club was founded in 1888, and since many employees of the Orient Steam Navigation Shipping Line – later taken over by P & O (Peninsular and Oriental) – had become involved, the name Orient was adopted on the suggestion of a player.

The name was appropriate for a club that played in East London. In 1898 they became Clapton Orient, adding the name of what was then a select London suburb with the aim of gaining added respectability. In 1937 the club moved further east in Leyton, becoming Leyton Orient in 1946.

Leyton means 'farmstead on the River Lea', which is nearby. 'Lea' is a Celtic river name possibly meaning 'light river'. In 1965 the area was absorbed into the new borough of Waltham Forest and the club dropped 'Leyton' from its name, but in 1987 they restored it to appeal to the local community.

Nickname: *The O's*
The nickname is taken from the first letter of the club name.

Ground: *Matchroom Stadium, Brisbane Road*
The *Matchroom Stadium,* named after the chairman Barry Hearn's stable of snooker players, was previously called *Leyton Stadium, Brisbane Road* (originally Osborne Road). It lies between Leyton High Road and Hackney Marshes, with the main entrance on Osborne Road. It was the home of Leyton FC, who first played there in September 1905. It became the works ground of the Bryant and May match factory in the 1920s until Leyton Amateurs returned in 1929. They played there until they were evicted by the council for rent arrears and were replaced by Clapton Orient in 1937.

The stand names are the standard *North, South, East* and *West.*

Crest

The main feature of the crest is two wyverns, mythical winged reptilian creatures. The wyvern is similar to the dragon as portrayed in European legends, but has only two legs and cannot breathe fire. In heraldry, they represent pestilence and conquest. These half-cragon, half-serpent creatures link the 'eastern mystery' of the Orient with the club's history in East London and its association with the Orient Shipping Line. The 'dragon' element of the wyvern may also represent the club's links with the City of London, whose crest is similar to Orient's, whereas the serpent symbolises the sea, another link to the Orient Shipping Line (see above).

It was not until 1946 that the club decided to put an official crest on the team's shirts, following the change of name (see above). The present badge dates from 1976, when a competition to design a new one was held in the local *Walthamstow Guardian* newspaper. Clive Brown and Mark Hodges were joint winners. The final design was completed by the club chairman Brian Winston.

The crest, which was altered slightly to include Leyton when the club changed its name back to Leyton Orient in 1987, also includes the team's year of formation, on a football.

Fanzine: *10p Pidgeon*

The Pidgeon is the last fanzine to be printed before each home game so as to catch the latest rumours and news that don't appear in the matchday programme.

Websites: *Orient ExpressNet 2004* www.orientexpressnet. co.uk), *O's Mad* (www.leytonorient-mad.co.uk), *Brisbane Road.com* (www.brisbaneroad.com)

Orient ExpressNet 2004 is a play on the name of the famous passenger train, the Express d'Orient or Orient Express. In 1876 a Belgian, Georges Nagelmackers, founded La Compagnie Internationale des Wagons-Lits to operate luxury sleeping and dining cars all over Europe. In 1883 the Express d'Orient started running twice a week on a route from Paris to Strasbourg, Munich, Vienna, Budapest, Bucharest and across the Danube to Ruse in Bulgaria. From there, passengers boarded a second train for the seven-hour journey to Varna on the Black Sea, from where a fourteen-hour sea voyage completed the journey to Constantinople (Istanbul). *O's Mad* refers to the team's nickname (see **Nickname**, above), and *Brisbane Road.com* is named after the ground.

Lincoln City

The club was formed in 1883 and named after the city. Lincoln's name comes from *lindon*, the Celtic word for 'pool' or 'lake', and refers to the marshy lands and broad pools formed by the River Witham which flows through the centre of the city. Brayford pool is still partly preserved. The Romans established a fortified town for retired legionaries there and added *colonia*, or 'colony', to the Latinised name Lindum. The first two parts of each word have combined to form the modern name.

Nickname: *The Red Imps*

Lincoln are known as the *Imps* (*Red*, from the team's colours) because of a tiny grotesque carving in Lincoln Cathedral at the top of the last complete column on the north side of the Angel Choir. James Ward Usher, a local jeweller and watchmaker, made a fortune by devising the legend of the Lincoln Imp, which he turned into the city's emblem in the 1880s. It is now also the county emblem of Lincolnshire. His story recounted how a couple of imps were hopping around the cathedral, until one of them was turned to stone for trying to talk to the angels carved into the roof of the choir. The other imp made a hasty retreat on the back of a witch. The wind is still supposed to haunt the cathedral awaiting their return. There are two red imps on the gates at the entrance to the club car park.

Ground: *Sincil Bank*

The club played at a ground called *John O'Gaunt's*, named after the medieval owner of a nearby house and stables. In 1894 City's land-lord died and his family sold up to builders. City had to move and chose *Sincil Bank*, which is named after Sincil Drain, a tree-lined canal that is thought to have been engineered by the Romans and ran behind John O'Gaunt's ground. It serves as an overflow from the River Witham.

The *Stacey West Stand* is dedicated to the memory of Bill Stacey and Jim West, two Lincoln fans who died in the fire at Bradford City's Valley Parade ground in 1985 (see **Bradford City**, Ground). The stand, opened in August 1990, used to be called the *Railway End* after the railway embankment which until 1990 formed the ground's northern boundary. However, the railway was closed and the club car park is now on the site of the old embankment. The *Main (St Andrew's) Stand* is so-called after St Andrews, a district east of the ground. The *IMPS Stand*, formerly the *South Park Stand* after the nearby park, is now sponsored by the Industrial and Marine Plant Supplies company, whose acronym, coincidentally, spells out the club's nickname. The *Co-Op Community Echo Stand* is named after the Co-Operative Society and *Lincolnshire Echo* newspaper that sponsor the stand. It was previously known as the *Linpave Stand*, after the local firm that built it, or *Sincil Bank Terrace*.

Crest

The current badge, showing the club's historic imp on a red cross, was first used in 1997 following John Beck's appointment as manager. He was keen to introduce a sense of community spirit within the club and felt the imp was a good symbol to represent the players. The imp first appeared on the badge in the 1971–2 season. The red cross and fleur-de-lis, which were taken from the city's coat of arms, had been removed towards the end of the 1960s.

The imp was itself removed in 1993, however, after a run of bad luck, including the 1985 Bradford City fire disaster in which fifty-six people died (see **Ground**, above), Lincoln's relegation to the Conference in 1987 and the death on the pitch of a 25-year-old York City player, David Longhurst, after he collapsed during a game against Lincoln at Bootham Crescent in 1990. When Lincoln won promotion to the Second Division (now League 1) in 1998 the club decided to mix the two previous crests and arrived at the current combination of cheeky yellow imp and red cross.

Fanzines: *Deranged Ferret, The Yellow Belly*

Deranged Ferret takes its name from a classic programme note by Lincoln's eccentric former manager Colin Murphy (1987–90) in which he said: 'It doesn't matter what you say to 'em before the game or on the night before, all that matters is that they go out at 3 p.m. and run around like deranged ferrets for an hour and a half and we win and then I'll 'ave done me job.' *Yellow Belly* is a famous nickname given to people from Lincolnshire, in honour of the county's regiment who wore yellow jerseys in battle.

Website: *Planet Imp* (www.lincolncity-mad.co.uk)

The website refers to the club's nickname (see **Nickname**, above).

Liverpool

Everton had been tenants at Anfield for eight years when in 1892 they had a dispute with their landlord, John Houlding, a wealthy local brewer. He wanted to raise their annual rent to £250, so the club left the ground and formed a new team on the other side of Stanley Park at Goodison Park. Houlding, who later became the city's mayor, then formed a new club. He tried to retain the name Everton but the Football League ruled against it and so he decided to call the team after the whole city, not just the local area. On 15 March 1892 he founded Liverpool Association FC.

'Liverpool' probably means 'livered pool', that is, one clotted with weeds. Liverpool is situated on the northern side of the Mersey estuary, and the pool was a former muddy creek of the Mersey, which has now been drained. Other origins of the name have been suggested, including 'elverpool', a reference to the large number of eels in the River Mersey. The mythical Liver bird was invented to explain the name and adopted as the emblem of the club and the city. The creature is thought to be an amalgamation of the thirteenth-century royal insignia adopted by King John and the cormorants which used to be found around Anfield. It can still be spotted atop the Liver Building, and at Liverpool John Moores University, constructed in bronze and stone.

Nicknames: *Reds, Pool*
Reds comes from the team colours, and *Pool* is taken from the club name.

Ground: *Anfield Road*
Liverpool first played at *Anfield*, named after the local suburb, on 1 September 1892. 'Anfield' is derived from 'Hanging Field' or 'Hangfield', which refers to the deeply sloping or hanging nature of the ground, although executions may have been carried out in the area during the mid-1700s. The hangings are thought to have taken place on London Road, which is closer to the city centre, but as the number increased a new location was needed. The area identified was a field by what is now Sleepers Hill at the bottom of Anfield Road, on the way up to Liverpool's ground. In ancient terms 'hang-

field' is a division of land, and both meanings became associated with the area. The name was shortened to Hangfield and many years later, as the area became more populated, was then altered slightly to Anfield.

The large south-end terrace, *Kop Stand*, was christened the *Spion Kop*, which means 'look-out hill' in Afrikaans, within weeks of its opening on 1 September 1906. The name was suggested by Ernest Edwards, the sports editor of the local *Post and Echo*, and the first mention of the Kop came in that newspaper a few days before a derby versus Everton on 29 September. Edwards proposed the name to commemorate a battle between Boer and British forces from 23 to 24 January 1900 during the Second Boer War (1899–1902) in the campaign to relieve Ladysmith, which resulted in a famous British defeat. The war in South Africa between the British and settlers of Dutch origin (called Boers, Afrikaners or Voortrekkers) put an end to the two independent republics the settlers had founded.

General Sir Charles Warren decided to attack the Boers along two fronts. On the night of 23 January he sent a force under Brigadier General Woodgate to secure Spion Kop, a rocky outcrop that appeared to be the key to the almost unprotected Boer right centre flank. The assault on the hill, situated along the Tugela River in Natal about 38 kilometres west-south-west of Ladysmith, was led by the 2nd Royal Lancaster Regiment and the 2nd Royal Lancashire Fusiliers.

When daylight came, the British forces discovered that the plateau they were on was in a vulnerable position and offered them little protection. The steepness of the hillside meant they had been unable to bring artillery, leaving them poorly prepared for the battle ahead. Exposed to Boer sharpshooters and artillery fire from all sides, some 322 British soldiers, many from Merseyside, were slaughtered and 563 wounded under heavy fire after a battle described by reporters, among them Winston Churchill, as an 'acre of massacre, that complete shambles'. There were 50 dead and 120 injured on the victorious Boer side. Afterwards, the open mounds on which Lancashire fans stood at football grounds became known as Spion Kops in memory of the tragedy.

The first Kop may not in fact have been at Anfield, as is widely believed, but at Arsenal's Manor Ground in 1904, although all foot-ball fans associate the Kop with Liverpool. The days of 28,000 supporters on one of the largest single-tier stands in the world, holding up red and white scarves and singing 'You'll Never Walk

Alone' as they swayed together, ended on 30 April 1994 with the move to an all-seater stadium. But the Kop will always be associated with the nostalgic memory of the club's heyday of the 1970s and 80s under Bill Shankly and his successor Bob Paisley (see below), when local folklore claimed that the fans could suck the ball into the goal if Liverpool were playing towards that end.

The *Centenary Stand*, formerly the *Kemlyn Road Stand*, is a new £8.5 million stand opened by the UEFA President Lennart Johansson on 1 September 1992, a hundred years after Liverpool played their first match at Anfield. The *Anfield Road Stand* is named after the road on which it stands.

Two pairs of wrought-iron gates stand at two entrances to the ground: the *Shankly Gates* – incorporating the words 'You'll Never Walk Alone', unveiled by Bill Shankly's widow Nessie in 1982 – and the *Paisley Gates*, each pair named after the club's greatest managers.

Crest
To honour the ninety-six Liverpool fans who died in the Hillsborough stadium disaster, the club decided to mark its centenary year in 1992 by incorporating into a new crest design the famous Kop anthem 'You'll Never Walk Alone' and two symbolic flames. The mythical Liver bird (see above) remains at the centre of the badge.

Fanzines: *The Liverpool Way, Another Wasted Corner, When Sunday Comes, Kopites, Kop Files, Red All Over the Land, All Day And All of the Night, Through the Wind and Rain*

The Liverpool Way refers to the pass and move style of play developed by Bill Shankly and Bob Paisley (see **Ground,** above) and the way in which the club and the fans conduct themselves. *Another Wasted Corner* harks back to the early 1990s, when the team was notoriously poor at taking corners. *When Sunday Comes* refers to the switch to Sunday games to satisfy the television schedules, lamenting the loss of regular Saturday fixtures. *Kopites* and *Kop Files* take their names from the famous Kop Stand (see **Ground,** above). *Red All Over the Land* (http://raotl.co.uk) is a play on the team's nickname and a lofty claim to the fanzine's circulation. *All Day And All of the Night* is the title of a song by The Kinks. *Through The Wind and Rain* (http://Liverpool.rivals.net) comes from two lines of the Liverpool supporters' anthem 'You'll Never Walk Alone', a song from the musical *Carousel*, written by R. Rodgers and O. Hammerstein II, which became a hit for Merseybeat group Gerry and the Pacemakers when they covered it in 1963:

> When you walk through a storm
> Hold your head up high,
> And don't be afraid of the dark...
> Walk on through the wind,
> Walk on through the rain,
> Though your dreams be tossed and blown,
> Walk on, walk on, with hope in your heart,
> And you'll never walk alone,
> You'll never walk alone.

Websites: *Kop Talk* (www.kop talk.com), *Red and White Kop* (www.redandwhitekop.net), *This is Anfield* (www. thisisanfield.com), *The Shankly Gates* (http://liverpool. rivals.net), *The Liverpool FC Bootroom Net* (www. lfcbootroom.net), *LiverWeb* (www.liverweb.org.uk)
Kop Talk and *Red and White Kop* are named after the famous Spion Kop stand (see **Ground**, above). *This is Anfield* refers to the words on the sign mounted by Bill Shankly on the wall above the exit from the players' tunnel to intimidate the opposition as they run on to the pitch. *The Shankly Gates* (incorporating *Pass and Move.com*) is named after the wrought-iron gates at the ground erected in honour of the club's great manager (see **Ground**, above). *The Liverpool FC Bootroom Net* is a celebration of the boot room at Anfield, a small kit room under the stand where the players' boots were stored. In the early years of the 1960s under Bill Shankly, the culture of the boot room was behind every success that followed in an unprecedented era of glory for the club. Early in Shankly's reign his assistants Bob Paisley and Joe Fagan began using the room as a makeshift office, having nowhere else to go. The club's management team would talk about strategy and tactics over cups of tea in the tiny room. A footballing dynasty had been conceived with its name taken from the boot room. *LiverWeb* is named after the mythical Liver bird, the emblem of the city and the club.

Luton Town

Luton Town FC was founded in 1885 by the amalgamation of two leading local clubs, Wanderers and a works team called Excelsior, at a meeting in Luton Town Hall. Three months earlier the Wanderers had changed their name to Luton Town Wanderers, and they were not happy about the formation of another club with 'Town' in its name. They were eventually persuaded to merge at the meeting, though. Luton Town became the first professional team south of Birmingham in 1890.

The Bedfordshire town has a name that means 'farmstead on the Lea', the Lea being the river on which it stands. The river's own Celtic name may mean 'bright one'. It is not clear how Luton came by its change of vowel from 'e' to 'u'.

Nicknames: *The Hatters, Strawplaiters*
The nicknames refer to Luton's traditional straw hat-making industry, although *Strawplaiters* is now rarely used as a nickname. The straw-plaiting industry was brought to Luton by a group of Scots under the protection of Sir John Napier of Luton Hoo.

Ground: *Kenilworth Road Stadium*
The club moved to its ground, originally called *Ivy Road* after the road on which it was situated, in 1905. The name *Kenilworth Road*, after the road that runs along one end of the ground, was adopted after the First World War, although the club's address is 1 Maple Road.

The *Kenilworth Road Stand* is named after the road on which it is situated, as is the *Oak Road Stand*. The *Bobbers Stand* has had this name since it was built in 1933, because it cost a bob (one shilling; 5p) to stand on the terrace. In 1985 the club stripped out the Bobbers Stand and installed a line of executive boxes, for the first time in the history of British football turning one whole side of the ground into a private viewing area for just 210 spectators.

Crest
The crest is based on the town's coat of arms, granted in 1876. The bee is the emblem of industry, the hive represents the straw-plaiting

for which Luton was famous (see **Nicknames**, above). The wheat-sheaf represents agriculture and the cultivation of wheat-straw, the rose is taken from the arms of the Napier family, and the thistle is a symbol of Scotland. The hand holding the bunch of wheat may be another symbol of straw-plaiting, or it may derive from the arms of John Whethamsteade, Abbot of St Albans, who in the fifteenth century rebuilt the chancel of St Mary's church in Luton. The straw hat at the top of the crest is again representative of the straw-plaiting industry.

Fanzine: *Mad as a Hatter*
Mad as a Hatter refers to the club's nickname, and light-heartedly the mental state of those supporting under-achieving Luton. It is taken from the character of the Mad Hatter in Lewis Carroll's story *Alice's Adventures in Wonderland*, which first appeared in 1865. Robert Crab, a seventeenth-century eccentric who lived at Chesham and gave all his goods to the poor, living on leaves and grass, is said to have been the original 'mad' hatter who gave rise to the expression. However, a researcher in the United States discovered that people working as hat-makers could have been affected by inhaling the vapours of the nitrate of mercury used to treat the felt used for hatmaking.

The phrase certainly existed long before Carroll's book, and may originate in the Anglo-Saxon word *atter*, meaning 'poison' (closely related to 'adder', the British snake whose bite can cause fever). In fact, Carroll himself may not have been thinking of a hatter but referring to a man notable for wearing a top hat. Carroll suggested to Sir John Tenniel, who drew the book's original illustrations, that the character should be like Theophilus Carter, a furniture dealer based near Oxford. He was possibly also a little mad: one of his inventions was an alarm-clock bed, displayed at the Great Exhibition in London, which tipped its occupant on to the floor when it was time to get up!

Websites: *Hatter Net* (www.hatter net.com), *Hatters Mad* (www.lutontown-mad.co.uk)
Hatter Net and *Hatters Mad* both refer to the club's nickname (see **Fanzine**, above).

Macclesfield Town

The club began playing football in 1874, having played rugby from the mid-nineteenth century. It was named after the Cheshire town whose own name means 'Maccel's open land'. The open land, Old English *feld*, was probably at one time part of a forest in the Peak District.

Nickname: *The Silkmen*
The nickname reflects the town's history as a centre for the manufacture of silk. In the late eighteenth and early nineteenth centuries Macclesfield was one of Britain's main silk spinning and weaving centres, its trade having boomed when French silks became unavailable during the Napoleonic Wars. The silk mills went into rapid decline after the 1940s when artificial fibres became available, leaving just a few manufacturers and two museums as testimony to the town's glorious past.

Ground: *Moss Rose*
The club moved to *Moss Rose* in 1891 when it was just a field on the north-eastern corner of a piece of land called Dane's Moss, close to London Road. The ground is named after the Moss Rose pub, which stands on a piece of land known as Moss Rose.

The *Estate Road (Alfred McAlpine) Stand* is named after the Moss Estate behind that end of the ground. The Alfred McAlpine construction company sponsors the stand. The name of the *Silkman End* derives from the club's nickname (see **Nickname**, above). The *Star Lane (HFS Loans) Stand* is named after the road behind the stand. HFS Loans sponsors the stand.

Crest
The badge shows a blue rampant lion holding a sheaf, probably derived from the arms of the Earls of Chester, and is taken from the town's coat of arms. Although Macclesfield is an ancient borough, it did not have a coat of arms until 1960.

Fanzine: *Ryan's Knob*
Ryan's Knob is named after part of the anatomy of the club's former

goalkeeper Ryan Price. In 1997 when the club won promotion to the Football League, the players celebrated in the Kettering dressing room at the end of the game. The *Macclesfield Express* photographer took a great picture of Ryan showing off his manhood that made the front page of that week's paper!

Websites: *The Silk Web* (http://macclesfieldtown.rivalsnet), *Silkmen Mad* (www.macclesfieldtown-mad.co.uk)
The Silk Web and *Silkmen Mad* are references to the team's nickname (see **Nickname,** above).

Manchester City

Manchester City was founded in 1880 when St Mark's Church, West Gorton, added a football section to its cricket club. The club merged with Gorton Athletic in 1884 to become Gorton FC. A change of ground brought another name change and it became Ardwick FC in 1887, before going bankrupt and being re-formed in 1894 as a limited company called Manchester City.

The club takes its name from the city, whose name indicates that it was once a walled Roman fort or town. 'Chester' comes from Old English *ceaster*, ultimately from the Latin *castra*, 'camp'. The Roman name of the settlement was Mamucium, probably from the Celtic word *mamma*, 'breast', describing the rounded hill on which the fort stood. The adjective Mancunian, meaning 'of Manchester', seems to have arisen from a miscopying of the Roman name.

Motto
Superbia in Proelio. Pride in Battle.

Nicknames: *Blues*, *Citizens*
Blues is a reference to the team's sky blue shirts; *Citizens* comes from the City part of the club name.

Ground: *City of Manchester Stadium*
The club moved from their old *Maine Road* ground to a new stadium in 2003. The *City of Manchester Stadium* is situated in East Manchester, about a mile from West Gorton, where City were founded in 1880 (see above). The club purchased the 48,000 seater stadium from Manchester City Council after the 2002 Commonwealth Games were held there. It is also known by the acronym *COMS*, and as *Eastlands* and *Sportcity*.

The *Colin Bell (West) Stand* is named after the former City and England midfield player Colin Bell. In 2003 every affiliated supporters club was invited to nominate a name for the West Stand, and the resulting shortlist was voted on by City fans on the club's website. The former manager Joe Mercer and Bell were the two clear contenders. A decision was taken to name the stand after Bell and the main pedestrian walkway to the new stadium, used by up to

30,000 fans at every home fixture, *Joe Mercer Way*.

Bell is widely held to be City's best ever player. He was nick-named 'King of the Kippax' after the *Kippax Stand* at the old Maine Road ground, renowned for its singing. He was part of the famous trio that also included Francis Lee and Mike Summerbee in City's most successful side during the 1960s and early 70s. They won the First Division (now Premier League) title in 1968, the FA Cup in 1969, the League Cup and European Cup Winners' Cup in 1970.

Bell made his debut for City in 1966 after joining from Bury, and stayed at the club until 1979. He won forty-eight England caps, more than any other City player, and featured in the 1970 World Cup finals in Mexico. In 1975, at the age of just 29, he was injured in a tackle with Manchester United's Martin Buchan during a League Cup match at Maine Road. Although he attempted a return in 1977 he was forced to retire in 1979 and is now a club ambassador.

Mercer was manager at City from 1965 to 1971, the most successful period in the team's history, helped by his fedora-wearing assistant Malcolm Allison. Mercer continued as general manager at the club until 1972.

The service road that encircles the stadium is called *Eastlands Way*, giving rise to the colloquial name for the stadium itself. *Commonwealth Way* commemorates the Commonwealth Games, for which the stadium was originally built. The main entrance in the stadium's *West Stand* is reached via *Citizens' Lane*, a reference to the club's nickname, and the route into the Sportcity complex, to the north of the stadium, is *Sportcity Way*. The other stands are called *North, South Key 103* and *East*. The Key 103 stand is named after the sponsor, a Manchester music station launched as Piccadilly Radio in 1974.

Crest

The latest design was unveiled in 1997. The golden eagle, used as a crest for the city of Manchester in 1957, has three stars above its head to provide a more continental feel. All that remains from the more traditional crest is the ship, which signifies Manchester's links with the rest of the world, above the initials MCFC and the club motto (see **Motto**, above).

Fanzines: *Bert Trautmann's Helmet, King of the Kippax, Chips 'n' Gravy, City Till I Cry*
Bert Trautmann's Helmet is named after the club's former German

goalkeeper, once a prisoner of war, who broke his neck in the 1956 FA Cup final but still played on. *King of the Kippax* comes from the Kippax Stand at City's old Maine Road ground. *Chips 'n' Gravy* is named after a local delicacy. *City Till I Cry* is a variation on the familiar terrace chant 'City Till I Die', reflecting the club's lack of success since the glory years of the late 1960s and early 1970s, culminating in relegation to the Second Division (now League 1) in 1999.

Websites: *Blue Moon* (**www.bluemoon-mcfc.co.uk**), *The Citizen* (**www.the-citizen.org.uk**)
Blue Moon is the title of the supporters' song:

> I said blue moon,
> You saw me standing alone,
> Without a dream in my heart,
> Without a love of my own...

The Citizen is a reference to the team's nickname (see **Nicknames,** above).

Manchester United

The club was founded as Newton Heath Lancashire and Yorkshire Cricket Club in 1878 by staff employed by the Lancashire and Yorkshire Railway Company. Two years later the name was simplified to Newton Heath. The club went bankrupt in 1902, but was relaunched with the help of a wealthy local brewer, John H. Davies, and renamed Manchester United. 'United' was used because of the club's union with a group of business investors led by Davies. It reflected a pooling of resources and the sense that all the members were pulling together to achieve the same goals. (For the origin of the city name see **Manchester City**).

Nickname: *Red Devils*
The Red Devil has its roots in Rugby League. Salford's Rugby League team remained unbeaten on their 1934 tour of France and the press dubbed them *Les Diables Rouges* – the Red Devils. After the Second World War United fans informally adopted the nickname for Sir Matt Busby's side. He even preferred it to the well-known nickname the 'Busby Babes' which was given to his outstanding team of young players, many of whom died in the Munich air crash of 1958.

Ground: *Old Trafford*
The site, not far from the Old Trafford cricket ground and five miles from United's original ground at *Bank Street*, Clayton, was bought by John H. Davies after United won their first League title in 1908. Trafford, now a metropolitan borough with a population of about 220,000 including the towns of Altrincham, Sale, Stretford and Urmston, has a name that means 'a ford on a Roman road'.

The stands are *Main*, *North* (formerly the *United Road Stand*), *West* (*Stretford End* after the local district) and *East Stand* (*Scoreboard End*, after the old manual scoreboard). The road to the ground, *Sir Matt Busby Way* (formerly Warwick Road) was named after United's illustrious European Cup-winning manager. He joined United as manager in 1945 and led the team to the First Division (now Premier League) title in 1952. The young side he developed, nicknamed the 'Busby Babes' and including players like Bobby

Charlton and Duncan Edwards, won the title in 1956 and 1957 when they were also FA Cup runners-up. In 1958 they were struck by tragedy when the plane carrying the squad home from a European Cup tie crashed on take-off at Munich, killing eight players. Busby recovered from serious injuries to rebuild the team with players like Denis Law and George Best. In 1968 they won the European Cup at Wembley, his biggest success. Busby was knighted and retired as manager in 1969. He remained at the club as a director until 1982.

Crest

The badge shows the Red Devil from the club's nickname. United used a crest derived from the City of Manchester's coat of arms for Cup finals throughout the 1950s and 1960s, and this is the origin of the ship on today's badge. By the late 1960s pirated merchandise was increasing and the Football Association advised clubs to copyright their crests in order to prevent black market trade. Since United could not own the city's coat of arms, the Red Devil was introduced for the 1969–70 season, thereby allowing the club to secure a brand image.

Mansfield Town

The club was formed by a Boys' Brigade as Mansfield Wesleyans in 1897 and changed its name to Mansfield Town in 1910.

The Nottinghamshire town is named after the River Maun on which it stands. The river's name comes from a hill some four miles away formerly called Mammesheud, meaning 'Man's headland'. Mam, the name of the hill itself, probably derives from *mamma*, 'breast', the same Celtic word that lies behind Manchester's name. The second half of the town's name is Old English *feld*, 'open land'.

Nicknames: *The Stags, The Yellows*

The Stags was first used in newspaper reports of the mid 1920s, probably because of the town's coat of arms, which includes a stag, and Mansfield's proximity to the deer in Sherwood Forest. At one time there was a tree in West Gate in the town centre with a plaque claiming it was the centre of the ancient Sherwood Forest. The tree disappeared some years ago, but the plaque still exists on the wall of a nearby solicitors' office.

Ground: *Field Mill*

In 1905 the club moved to Field Mill, which is named after a cotton mill built in 1797 by the Duke of Portland. Before it was demolished in 1925 it was situated on the opposite side of Quarry Lane from the present ground. The nearby Early Doors pub was originally Mill Field House, home of the Greenhalgh family who ran the mill until 1901. In 1861 four of the Greenhalgh brothers formed the Greenhalgh Football Club whose team played at Mill Field, making the ground the second oldest in the world after Hallam FC's Sandygate in Sheffield (1860). In the 1880s the two words became transposed, and the name Field Mill came in to popular use.

The stands are called the *West Stand, Quarry Lane (South) Stand, Bishop Street Stand* and the *North Stand*.

Crest

The club crest has always been a stag's head. It was first used on the shirts worn in the 1954–5 season and is taken from the team's nickname (see **Nicknames**, above). The current crest shows the outline of a stag's head in profile, on a shield, in the club's amber and blue colours.

Fanzines: *Follow the Yellow Brick Road, Deja Vu*
Follow the Yellow Brick Road (www.dejavu.fanzine.btinternet.co. uk/index2.html) is a reference to the team's amber shirts. The title is taken from the yellow brick road in the Land of Oz along which Dorothy travels with her friends in the 1939 musical film *The Wizard of Oz*, starring Judy Garland.

Websites: *Stags Online* (**http://mansfieldtown.rivals.net**),
Stags Net (**www.stagsnet.net**)
Stags Online and *Stags Net* refer to the team's nickname (see **Nicknames**, above).

Middlesbrough

The formation of Middlesbrough FC was first discussed at a tripe supper at the Corporation Hotel in 1875 but the club was not formally established until a meeting at the Talbot Hotel the following February.

The name of the town and port in Cleveland means 'middle forti-fied place' from Old English *midleste* or 'middlemost' and *burh* or 'fort'. It is not clear why the fort was 'middlemost'. It may have been a resting place for travellers in medieval times halfway between St Cuthbert's monastery at Durham and St Hilda's at Whitby, or 'middle' could simply have been the name of a district, with the River Tees, on which Middlesbrough stands, as its northern boundary.

Nicknames: *The Boro, Ironsides*
Boro comes from the team name. *Ironsides* is a reference to the area's heavy industries.

Ground: *The Riverside Stadium*
Middlesbrough played their first match at this stadium, named by the supporters after the dockland area in which it is situated, in 1995, after moving from *Ayresome Park*, which was named after the local district. The approach to the *Riverside Stadium* on the west side is called *Ayresome Boulevard*, after the old ground. Although the Riverside fronts onto the former Middlesbrough Dock, the mouth of the dock with the River Tees is behind the North Stand so it is as much a riverside as a dockside ground.

The stands are simply called *North, South, East* and *West*.

Crest
The badge shows a lion and the date 1986, when the club was re-formed as Middlesbrough FC after being declared bankrupt. The club had previously been known as Middlesbrough Football and Athletic Club. After it went into receivership, a new identity was needed to distinguish it from the former organisation, and a new crest was designed by the club's programme producers Hillprint. The rampant lion, which is also used by the local rugby and cricket clubs, is taken from the coat of arms of the local Brus family. The

town was incorporated as a borough in 1853, and immediately adopted a coat of arms which included the rampant lion, although it was not registered with the college of arms until 1911.

Fanzine: *Fly Me to the Moon*

Fly Me to the Moon comes from a statement made by former manager Bruce Rioch, after an inspirational performance by Boro's tough central defender Tony Mowbray in a 2–2 draw with Everton in an FA Cup tie in 1988: 'If I had to fly to the moon I'd take Tony Mowbray, my captain, with me. He's a magnificent man.' Everton won the replay with an own goal – by Mowbray – but the tribute followed the defender around. Mowbray had come up through the ranks at the club after signing as an apprentice in 1981. He was sold for £1 million ten years later, having helped Boro to successive promotions from the Third to the old First Division (Premier League) before they were relegated. He made 419 appearances and scored 30 goals for the club. *Fly Me to the Moon*, which started in 1988, also has a website (www.middlesbrough.rivals.net).

Millwall

The club was formed in 1885 as Millwall Rovers by employees of Morton's Cannery and Preserve Works, often referred to as Morton's jam and marmalade factory, in East Ferry Road. Most of the workers were Scots who had moved to London. The team began life in the docklands of Millwall, which form the southern district of the Isle of Dogs peninsula in London, by the River Thames, and were soon nicknamed the Dockers.

The Millwall area takes its name from mills that stood there until the eighteenth century. The 'wall' was a riverside embankment. The club replaced 'Rovers' with 'Athletic' in 1889. After moving south of the river to the Den in the more densely populated district of Bermondsey in 1910, it became simply Millwall in 1925.

Nickname: *The Lions*
Millwall were dubbed 'The Lions of the South' by the newspapers during their giant-killing FA Cup run in the 1899–1900 season, when as a Southern League club they got past the qualifying rounds for the first time before beating Jarrow, Queen's Park Rangers and the League champions Aston Villa after two replays. The *Lions* nickname stuck because the image was so popular with cartoonists, who were employed to illustrate reports and articles at that time, rather than photographers. It may even have been originally picked up by the newspapers from shouts of 'Come on you Lions' by Millwall fans at a time when all things African were in vogue because of the Boer War – the chant may have been inspired by the heroics of the troops in South Africa. The same sentiments led to the open ends at several grounds being named Spion Kop (see **Liverpool**, Ground).

Millwall's Cup run came to an end in the semi-final with a 3–0 defeat in a replay against fellow Southern League side Southampton, who lost 4–0 to Bury in the final.

Ground: *The New Den*
The New Den takes its name from the club's previous ground the Den, in Cold Blow Lane, which was so called because it was the home of the Lions. In 1993, after eighty-three years, Millwall left

the Den and moved to the £16 million 20,000 all-seater stadium at *Senegal Fields*, named after a nearby street of terraced houses called Senegal Road. The new stadium is a quarter of a mile away from the Den. The stands are named *North, South (Cold Blow Lane End), East* and *West*. The name of the Cold Blow Lane End comes from the club's old ground, so-called because of its exposure to cold winds. 'Never did a name… express the character of a ground more accurately', wrote Simon Inglis in his *Football Grounds of Britain*.

Crest
Millwall's crest has always been based around the club's nickname and shows two red lions on their hind legs facing each other above a Millwall FC banner. The crest originally symbolised a Scottish lion because of the club's connections with the Scots who worked at the Morton's jam factory (see above, and **Fanzines**, below).

Fanzines: *Out of the Blue, The Lion Roars, No One Likes Us, Tales from Senegal Fields*
Out of the Blue is a reference to the team's blue and white strip, which was modelled on Scotland's colours because most of the players were of Scottish descent when the club was formed. *The Lion Roars* comes from the team nickname. *No One Likes Us* is a supporters' anthem based on the tune to Rod Stewart's 'Sailing': 'We are Millwall, we are Millwall, / No one likes us, we don't care'. *Tales from Senegal Fields* is named after the site of the New Den, which used to be playing fields.

MK Dons (Wimbledon)

Old boys from Central School formed the club as Wimbledon Old Centrals in 1889. The name was changed to Wimbledon in 1905, since by then most of the players were no longer associated with the school. The club ceased to exist for a short time in 1910 and then re-emerged in 1912, after combining with Wimbledon Borough.

The well-known district in south London has a name meaning 'Wynnmann's hill'. 'Don' derives from Old English *dun*, or 'hill'. The first part of the name was changed to 'Wymbanl' by the Normans, who found 'Wynnmann' difficult to pronounce.

The club changed its name to Milton Keynes (MK) Dons in 2004 following a controversial move in September 2003 to a temporary new home at the National Hockey Stadium in Milton Keynes, fifty miles north of Wimbledon. The club had gone into administration with debts of more than £20 million but the temporary stadium was developed after a businessman, Pete Winkelman, made funds available.

Milton Keynes, a high technology 'city' in Buckinghamshire designated in 1967 as Britain's largest new town, incorporated thirteen existing villages, notably Fenny Stratford, Bletchley, Wolverton and Stony Stratford. These old communities have been left virtually intact but are now an appendage to the industrial and commercial nucleus, encircled by a web of bypasses. The conurbation covers an area of almost fifty square miles and retains the name of a former village there. 'Milton' is derived from 'Middletone', which means 'middle farm', while 'Keynes' comes from Lucas de Kaynes, the Norman lord of the manor in the twelfth century who was from Cahaignes, near Caen, in northern France.

Nicknames: *The Dons, The Crazy Gang, Wombles*
Dons is an abbreviation of Wimbledon. *Crazy Gang*, a reference to the eccentric comedy team of the 1940s, was adopted by the celebrated Wimbledon squads of the 1980s and 90s. The team that won the FA Cup in 1988 with a shock 1–0 win over the favourites, Liverpool, were given the nickname because of the various non-League habits they brought with them on their meteoric rise to the First Division (Premier League) and the refreshingly unconven-

tional style adopted by managers like Dave Bassett, Bobby Gould and Joe Kinnear. The players responsible for their reputation included Dave Beasant, the first goalkeeper to save a penalty in a Wembley final when he denied John Aldridge, striker Alan Cork, hard-man midfielder Vinnie Jones (now an actor), goalscorer Lawrie Sanchez (currently Northern Ireland's manager), and Dennis Wise (the present Millwall player-manager). *Wombles* is a reference to the fluffy grey creatures in a children's television series who scoured Wimbledon Common, where Wimbledon once played, picking up litter.

Ground: *The National Hockey Stadium*
The club is using the hockey stadium temporarily until a new 28,000 all-seater stadium is built in conjunction with a major supermarket at Denbeigh. At the time of writing, it is planned that the new stadium will be ready for the start of the 2006–7 season. In 1991 the club was forced to leave its old *Plough Lane* home, where it had been based since 1912, because there was no prospect of the ground being redeveloped to meet the requirements of the Taylor Report. After sharing Crystal Palace's Selhurst Park ground, Wimbledon moved to Milton Keynes under new owners.

The Hockey Stadium stands are *North*, *South*, *East* and *West*.

Crest
The modern badge was designed by a local company and introduced after the club formally emerged from administration under a new name and ownership on 1 July 2004 (see above). The 'M' of the name sits on top of a sideways 'K' to create a chevron. The full name, MK Dons, is shown vertically to the left of the chevron. The Roman numerals MMIV (2004, the year the club changed its name) are included at the bottom of the crest.

Fanzine: *MOO*
MOO refers to Milton Keynes' famous concrete cow sculptures, a reflection of the environment at the club's new home in the new town. It replaced *It's Been Emotional*, which referred to the club's agonising departure from their historical home in Wimbledon.

Newcastle United

The club was founded in 1881 in the Byker district of Newcastle and was first called Stanley, before adopting the name Newcastle East End in October 1882 to avoid confusion with two other local clubs. East End played at Heaton, to the east of the city. In May 1892 their deadly local rivals Newcastle West End, who played on Town Moor to the west of the city, folded and East End took over the lease at their more accessible ground, which soon became known as St James' Park (see **Ground**, below). The club also changed its name to United since West and East had effectively become one team.

The city's name refers to the 'new castle' – actually a wooden fort – built by Robert Curthose, the bastard son of William the Conqueror's eldest son, in 1080. Newcastle was a Roman garrison station on Hadrian's Wall and the castle was built on the site of the former Roman fort. The present castle keep dates from the twelfth century, although little remains of the outer fortifications except the Black Gate, which was added in 1242 at a cost of £500.

Nickname: *The Magpies*
The nickname is a reference to the team's black and white shirts, which recall the black and white plumage of a magpie.

Ground: *St James' Park*
The ground is named after nearby St James' terrace – which, unusually, does not take an 's' after the apostrophe.

The *Gallowgate End (Newcastle Brown (South) Stand)* is named after the main thoroughfare behind the stand, called the Gallowgate because in the nineteenth century the area was the scene of hangings. The execution of one notorious female murderer drew a crowd of 20,000 in 1829. The last hanging was in 1844. The *Sir John Hall (North) Stand* (formerly *Leazes Terrace* or *Park End*) was the first of the club's new stands. It was built in 1993 and named after the club's former chairman, who is best known as the developer of Britain's largest shopping complex, the massive MetroCentre in Gateshead. Leazes Terrace takes its name from a row of elegant Georgian houses along the eastern side of Town Moor. It was part of a larger Georgian development for the gentry built in 1829. The *Milburn (West) Stand* was named after the late Jackie Milburn, United's much-loved and speedy centre forward, in 1990, two years after it had opened. 'Wor Jackie' scored 179 goals in 354 games for the club from 1944 to 1957. His death on 9 October 1988 brought thousands on to the streets for what was almost a state funeral. His statue now stands in the city centre.

Crest
The current badge, designed in 1988, is modelled on the coat of arms of Newcastle upon Tyne. The two seahorses represent Tyneside's strong correction with the sea, while the castle links the crest to the city's Norman keep. The black and white shield reflects the team's striped shirts. The flag, similar to that on the city crest, is a version of the cross of St George.

Fanzines: *True Faith, The Mag*
True Faith is what Newcastle supporters have in abundance as they devotedly support their team. *The Mag* is a shortened version of the club's nickname the Magpies.

Websites: *Talk of the Tyne* (www.talkofthetyne.com), *Tyne Talk* (www.tyne-talk.tk), *Newcastle Online* (www.newcastle-online.com), *Toonweb* (www.toonweb.co.uk), *Dr Gloom* (http://drgloom.co.uk)
Talk of the Tyne, a variation on the saying 'Talk of the Town' and the name of the river, began life as a fanzine called *Talk of the Toon* in 1991. The name was changed for the start of the 1994–5 season because Newcastle registered the name *Toon*. *Tyne Talk* also refers to the river. *Newcastle Online* is a joint venture between *Toon-Chat* and *Howay the Toon*, the latter being a variation on the local terrace chant *Howay the Lads*. *Howay* and *toon* are local dialect for 'away' and 'town' – the term is also used in *Toonweb*.

Dr Gloom has supported Newcastle for over forty years, during which time he has changed from the optimistic young lad who firmly believed each season was going to be 'our year', into the doom-laden figure of today, convinced Newcastle are destined never to win a domestic trophy. Even at the height of Kevin Keegan's managerial era, when the team were 12 points clear at the top of the Premier League, his was the lone voice saying they would not win the title. Sadly he was correct. Dr Gloom gives his prediction and a post mortem for each match.

Northampton Town

The club was founded in 1897 at Northamptonshire County Cricket Ground by schoolteachers connected with the Northampton and District Elementary Schools' Association.

The county town was originally known as Hampton, meaning 'home farm'. It added 'North' to distinguish itself from its southern namesake, Southampton, also originally Hampton, though with a different meaning (see **Southampton**).

Nickname: *The Cobblers*
The nickname is reference to the town's long history of shoe manufacturing. Many of the streets around the club's old County Ground, which it shared with Northamptonshire County Cricket Club, housed workers from the nearby Manfield shoe factory.

Ground: *Sixfields Stadium*
The stadium was opened in 1994 as part of a 65-acre redevelopment site at Duston. It cost £5.25 million plus about £6 million in infrastructure costs. Its name was chosen as the winning entry in a competition run by the *Chronicle and Echo* newspaper in January 1994. The winner, Alan Chamberlain, used to swim at Six Fields as a boy. Six Fields is the traditional name for the area.

The *Alwyn Hargrave Family (East) Stand* is named after the councillor who was instrumental in the planning of the move to the new stadium. The *Dave Bowen (North) Stand* is named after the club's former Welsh international, who had two spells as manager. Bowen was born in 1928 in Maesteg, Wales and won nineteen caps. He made thirty-five appearances for Northampton before becoming manager from 1959 to 1967 and again from 1969 to 1972. He then took over as general manager and secretary until 1985, when he joined the board. Bowen, who also managed Wales, died in 1995. The other stands are the *South* and *West*.

Crest
The badge is based on the town's coat of arms. The rose has been used as the emblem of Northamptonshire since at least 1665. The keep represents the castle built in the old Saxon town in about 1100,

soon after the Norman Conquest, by Simon de Senlis, the first Earl of Northampton. The castle became a favourite stopping off point for travelling royalty and was the site of several great councils and parliaments until 1380 when the town lost its importance. Northampton witnessed the trial of Thomas a Becket at the castle in 1164 and William Shakespeare set the first scene of *King John* in its great hall. Northampton sided with Parliament during the Civil War and one of Charles II's first acts was to raze its castle and walls. Northampton Castle station, near the site of the castle, preserves its name. The club badge includes a griffin standing as a supporter on the left of the castle keep, with an English lion rampant on the right. A griffin is a mythical creature with an eagle's head and wings and a lion's body. The club mascot is Clarence the Griffin.

Fanzines: *Hotel Ender, A Load of Cobblers, Fields Are Green*
Hotel Ender is named after the popular covered home supporters' Hotel End at the club's old County Ground, which was itself named after the County Hotel pub. *A Load of Cobblers* has a double meaning, suggesting the team nickname and the slang for nonsense or rubbish. 'Cobblers', short for 'cobblers awls', is rhyming slang for balls. An awl is a small pointed tool used by shoemakers. *Fields Are Green* is a supporters' song to the tune of 'The Red Flag'. It was voted the best football anthem by *Match of the Day* magazine readers:

> The fields are green the sky is blue
> The River Nene goes winding through
> The Market Square all cobble-stones
> It shakes the old dears to the bones.

> A finer town there'll never be
> A finer team you'll never see
> Big City lights don't bother me
> Northampton Town I'm proud to be.

Websites: *Cobblers Mad* (www.northamptontown-mad. co.uk)
Cobblers Mad refers to the team nickname (see **Fanzines** and **Nickname**, above).

Norwich City

The club was formed in 1902, largely through the initiative of two local schoolteachers who called a meeting at the Criterion Café. The club, which turned professional in 1905 after a meeting at the Agricultural Hall, is named after the county town of Norfolk.

'Norwich' means 'northern harbour or trading centre' from Old English *north* and *wic* or 'port'.

Nickname: *The Canaries*

The association with canaries comes from the French Huguenot refugees who arrived in the city in the sixteenth century to work as weavers in the local textile industry, helping to make Norwich the second-richest city in England after London at that time. They kept pet birds, including imported canaries, which they bred. By 1905 the pastime was becoming associated with Norwich City, and their former nickname, *Citizens*, began to be replaced by *Canaries*. Soon after, the decision was taken to play in yellow shirts, to reflect this nickname.

Ground: *Carrow Road*

The ground originally belonged to the mustard manufacturers Colmans, whose works lay to the east and who had bought it in 1870 for grazing work-horses. In 1935 Norwich moved to the ground, which is named after Carrow Priory, a Benedictine convent built around 525, some of whose ruins remain. Carrow is one of the eight villages that over the centuries merged into Norwich.

The *South (Jarrold) Stand* is named not because of its position, which lies more to the east, but after Arthur South, who had been Lord Mayor when he was persuaded to spearhead the club's revival in 1957. He became chairman in 1973 and was knighted the year after. The stand is sponsored by Jarrold, a local department store. *The Norwich and Peterborough River End Stand* is named after the River Wensum, which runs behind the stand. The Norwich and Peterborough Building Society sponsors the stand. The *Geoffrey Watling (City) Stand* commemorates the former chairman Geoffrey Watling, who was 'Mr Norwich City'. He saved the club from near bankruptcy, before presiding over their League Cup triumph in 1962 and helping to buy out the unpopular chairman Robert Chase in 1996. He then sold his majority shareholding to the current club owners Delia Smith and Michael Wynn-Jones. He died in 2004. The *Barclay End Stand* was originally called the *Station End* because it was nearest to the Norwich railway station. It was renamed after Captain Evelyn Barclay, a vice-president of the club and member of the banking family which has strong connections to the area. He donated the money to pay for the first terrace cover to be built in 1937.

Crest
When Norwich turned professional they adopted yellow and green as their colours and a canary as the club badge. In 1971 the local *Eastern Evening News* launched a competition for a new design, which was won by Tim Watson. His badge depicted the canary perched on a football, with Norwich's eleventh-century castle, one of the city's most prominent buildings, in the corner, guarded by a lion outside the main gate.

Websites: *On The Ball City* (www.norwichcity-mad.co.uk), *Wrath of the Barclay* (www.wrathofthebarclay.co.uk), *Canary Corner* (http://norwichcity.rivals.net), *Citizens 2 Canaries* (www.citizens2canaries.com)
'On The Ball City' is the title of a music hall song written by Albert T. Smith in about 1890. The song was taken up by Norwich fans shortly after the club was founded and is claimed to be the oldest football anthem still regularly heard at football grounds:

> Kick-off, throw it in, have a little scrimmage,
> Keep it low, a splendid rush, bravo, win or die,
> On the ball, City, never mind the danger,
> Steady on, now's your chance,
> Hurrah! We've scored a goal.

It was first mentioned in the *Eastern Daily Press* in 1905, although City probably inherited it from older Norwich teams such as Swans. *Wrath of the Barclay* reflects the history of the Barclay End, where traditionally the loudest fans sit. It used to be a terrace that held home and away supporters, leading to verbal sparring between fans. *Canary Corner* and *Citizens 2 Canaries* refer to the team nickname (see **Nickname**, above).

Nottingham Forest

Nottingham Forest Football club was formed at a meeting in the Clinton Arms in 1865. Forest are one of only two professional English teams named after the ground at which they were formed (the other is Crystal Palace). The Forest Racecourse, now Forest Recreation Ground, was an open area to the west of the city named after Sherwood Forest, the legendary home of Robin Hood and his Merry Men.

The county town of Nottingham has a name meaning 'homestead of Snot's people' with the initial S of the personal name dropped by the Normans, who found it difficult to pronounce 'Sn'.

Nicknames: *Reds*
The nickname is a reference to the team's colours. At the meeting in the Clinton Arms when the club was founded (see above) it was resolved to buy a dozen red caps, complete with tassels, thereby establishing the official club colour as 'Garibaldi Red'. The colour was named after Giuseppe Garibaldi (1807–82), the leader of the Italian freedom fighters known as the Redshirts, who were popular in England at the time. In 1860, at the head of his 1,000-strong Redshirts, Garibaldi conquered Sicily and Naples for the new kingdom of Italy.

Ground: *The City Ground*
In 1898, Forest moved a couple of hundred yards across the river from the *Town Ground* (named after the Town Arms pub) to settle at the *City Ground* in the district of West Bridgford, next door to the cricket ground at Trent Bridge where Notts County had played since 1883 (see **Notts County**, Ground). Nottingham was granted its charter as a city in 1897, and the City ground was named to commemorate the honour. County moved in the opposite direction in 1910, to Meadow Lane. Of all the English League clubs, Forest and County are the closest together: just 400 yards and the River Trent separate their grounds.

The *Trent End Stand* is named after the well-known Midlands river that runs behind the stand. The *Brian Clough (East) Stand* was formerly known as the *Executive Stand* but is now named after the club's celebrated, if controversial, manager who opened the £2.5 million stand in 1980. Clough managed Forest from 1975 to 1993, becoming the longest-serving manager in contemporary British football and celebrating over a thousand games as a manager. (The feat was matched by Manchester United's Alex Ferguson in 2004.) Clough took over a fairly ordinary side and steered them into the top flight in 1977. They won the League Cup and the championship the next season, making Clough the only manager apart from Herbert Chapman to win the League title with two clubs. In 1978–9 they were League runners-up and won the European Cup and League Cup, again, before successfully defending their European crown the following term after losing the League Cup final. Two more League Cup successes followed in 1989 and 1990, and they were runners-up in the FA Cup in 1991 and in the League Cup once more in 1992. It was a remarkable managerial record. The following year Forest were relegated, in Clough's final season before his retirement. He died in 2004. The *Bridgford Stand* is named after the local district.

Crest
The crest was created in 1973. It was designed by David Lewis, who won a competition organised by the *Nottingham Evening Post*. Sherwood Forest is represented on the badge by a tree, and the wavy design at the base depicts the River Trent above the word 'Forest'.

Fanzine: *Blooming Forest*
The fanzine's title plays on the two meanings of 'blooming': flowering, and as an expletive. The website is at http://nottinghamforest. rivals.net.

Website: *Lost That Loving Feeling* (www.ltlf.co.uk)
The website is named after a Righteous Brothers song of the same title. It is sung at the opposition by Forest fans whenever the team score. When the website was set up in 1999, Forest had just been relegated from the Premier League so the title was an accurate summary of the feelings around the club at that time:

> You've lost that loving feeling
> Oh, that loving feeling
> You've lost that loving feeling
> Now it's gone, gone, gone…

Notts County

The oldest team in the League, Notts County was formed in 1862 as the Notts Foot Ball Club, although it was not properly organised until a meeting at the George IV Hotel in 1864. Notts was a sporting club for 'county gentlemen' as the second word of the name indicates. Notts is a short form of the name of the county (see **Nottingham Forest**), cleverly used so that the club could call themselves 'County', which was rarely allowed by the local authorities.

Nickname: *Magpies*
Notts County have been known as the *Magpies* since 1890 when they became a limited company and changed their kit from chocolate and blue to the black and white striped shirts that resemble the colours of a magpie.

Ground: *Meadow Lane*
The club moved to *Meadow Lane* in 1910 after crossing the river from the Trent Bridge cricket ground where they had played since 1883. Meadow Lane was originally open ground next to a cattle market. The nearby *Iremonger Road* behind the Spion Kop is named after the club's celebrated goalkeeper Albert Iremonger, who made a record 601 appearances between 1905 and 1926.

The *Derek Pavis (Main) Stand* is named after a former Forest director who made his fortune from various heating, plumbing and other ventures. He fell out with then-Forest manager Brian Clough in 1984 and took over struggling Notts County in 1987, helping to transform Meadow Lane into a modern all-seater stadium. The *Jimmy Sirrel* or *County Road Stand* is named after the former manager who arrived at the club in November 1969 when the team had finished nineteenth in the Fourth Division (now League 2) the previous season. 'Ask any kid what he knows about Notts County and he'll tell you they're the "Oldest Football Team in the World". By the time I've finished he'll know a lot more,' Sirrel said when he took over. Within six years he had guided them into the First Division (now Premier League). He is regarded by many supporters as the best manager County have ever had. The *Kop Stand* is named after the Spion Kop (see **Liverpool**, Ground), and the *Meadow Lane*

(Family) Stand takes its name from the nearby road.

Crest
The badge, which shows two magpies on top of a ball, was first intro-duced in the 1986–7 season when the club was taken over by Derek Pavis (see **Ground**, above), although there had been a magpie on the club's first emblem in 1923. Underneath the magpies is the date of the club's foundation, 1862, proclaiming its heritage as the oldest League team in the world. The yellow colour which forms the back-ground has been associated with the club since former manager Neil Warnock introduced it in 1989. The current crest was introduced for the 2004–5 season to represent a new era after the club had come through administration and the threat of expulsion from the Football League.

Fanzine: *The Pie*
The Pie is a reference to the club's nickname (see **Nickname**, above).

Websites: *You Pies* (www.youpies.co.uk), *The Mighty Magpies* (www.nottscountyfc.cjb.net), *Up the Magpies* (http://homepage.ntlworld.com/carousel/maggies.html)
The names of the websites all refer to the club's nickname (see **Nickname**, above).

Oldham Athletic

In 1895 John Garland, the landlord of the Featherstall and Junction Hotel, formed a club called Pine Villa, named after Pine Mill, close to where they played their first game. Four years later the local professional club Oldham County went out of business and one of the liquidators persuaded Pine Villa to take over their athletic ground and change their name to Oldham Athletic to reflect the name of their new home.

The Lancashire town near Manchester has a name meaning 'old promontory' from the Old Norse *holmer*. The 'island' or 'promontory' in question is the spur at the western edge of Saddleworth Moor on which Oldham is situated. 'Old' was used simply because people had been living there a long time.

Nickname: *The Latics*
The nickname is an abbreviation of the world 'athletic'.

Ground: *Boundary Park*
When Oldham County folded in 1899 (see above) Pine Villa took over the ground but fell out with the landlord and moved to *Hudson Field*, a few hundred yards away. As local interest in Oldham Athletic grew the club decided in 1906 to return to the more spacious athletic ground, which later became known as *Boundary Park*.

It is so called because it lies on the municipal boundary of Oldham and Chadderton. The nearby Oldham Royal Hospital was formerly known as Boundary Park hospital. As far as anyone knows, there was no park there so the name must be the generic one used for a field or pitch.

The *Broadway Stand* takes its name from the road that lies about 100 yards behind the ground and which runs from Hollinwood to Royton. The *Main (Pukka Pies) Stand* is named after the Leicestershire-based sponsors. The *Chadderton Road (SSL International) Stand* is known locally as the *Chaddy End* after nearby Chadderton Way. It is sponsored by Seton, a locally-based medical supplies firm. The *Rochdale Road (Slumberland Dunlopillo) Stand* is named after the locally based sponsor and a main route between Oldham and Rochdale, which is close to that end of the ground.

Rochdale's Spotland stadium is six miles to the north.

Crest

The badge shows an owl on top of a football. It was redesigned in the 1980s by Stewart Beckett, a graphic designer and author of the club history *The Team From a Town of Chimneys*, who has been a lifelong fan. He turned the owl from side-on to face the viewer and also added the blue and red colours seen today.

The owl is derived from the town crest, based on the former arms of Oldham, which in turn originated in the arms of the Oldham family, showing three white owls (a pun on 'Owldham', see below) The link to the owl is also reflected in the former Oldham motto *Sapere Aude*, meaning 'Dare To Be Wise', which like the owls contains a play on the name. *Aude* contains the syllable 'Owd', suggesting the local pronunciation of 'Owdham' or 'Owldham'

The club's mascot is an owl called Chaddy, an abbreviation of the home fans' Chadderton Road End of the ground, known locally as the Chaddy End (see **Ground**, above).

Fanzine: *Beyond the Boundary*

The name of the fanzine is a reference to the ground name.

Website: *Latics Mad* (www.oldhamathletic-mad.co.uk)

The website is a reference to the club's nickname (see **Nickname**, above).

Oxford United

The club was founded by a doctor and a vicar at the Britannia Inn in 1893. It was originally called Headington, adding 'United' a year later. The club was not called Oxford United until 1960.

The university city was originally a market town named after the local ford where oxen could get over the River Thames, which runs through Oxfordshire. The ford is thought to have stood just below Folly Bridge, south of the city, although it may have been at Hinksey Ferry to the west.

Nickname: *The U's*
The nickname refers to the 'U' of 'United'.

Ground: *The Kassam Stadium*
Oxford United's ground is named after their chairman, Firoz Kassam, who arrived in Britain in the 1950s as a student from Tanzania, where he was born to Asian parents. His first job was washing up in an Indian takeaway. He opened a fish and chip shop in Brighton in 1970 and then borrowed money to acquire buildings in London to let to homeless families. He expanded into the hotel business, opening the Holiday Inn at Kings Cross in London in the mid-1990s. Kassam took control of Oxford in April 1999 when he acquired the 89.5 per cent majority shareholding for £1 million from their former chairman Robin Herd and took over the club's debts.

The stadium is situated on the outskirts of Oxford near the city's southern ring road at Minchery Farm. This ceased to be a working farm some time ago: back in the late 1970s and early 80s it had been a nightclub. The farmhouse was listed and there had been plans to revive it as a family pub but the buildings became derelict. In 2001 an arson attack destroyed any usefulness they may have had.

The stands in the three-sided stadium, opened on 18 August 2001, are named *North*, *East* (*Oxford Mail*, after the local newspaper that sponsors it) and *South*. Foundations are in place for the construction of a *West Stand*.

Crest
The crest shows an ox, represented by its head, crossing a ford,

reflecting the city and club name. The current crest was created in 2001 by the steward, Rob Alderman, to coincide with the club's move from the Manor Ground to the Kassam Stadium. The ox remains appropriate since the new ground is at Minchery Farm, even though there is no longer a farm in existence.

Fanzines: *Rage On, Yellow Fever*
Rage On was started in 1988 as *Raging Bull*, named after the Robert De Niro film and because of the club's association with oxen. New editors decided to change the name and held a competition but none of the entries appealed. With just a couple of hours to go before the deadline for the next fanzine to be printed, one of them, Martin Brodetsky, came up with *Rage On*, 'more out of desperation than anything, although we liked it because it maintained some sort of link with the previous name'. The website is *Rage Online* (www.rage online.co.uk). *Yellow Fever* reflects the colour of the team's shirts.

Websites: *Minchery Farm Web* (**www.mincheryfarm. plus.com**), *U's Mad* (**www.oxfordutd-mad.co.uk**)
Minchery Farm Web is named after the site on which the Kassam Stadium stands. *U's Mad* refers to the club's nickname (see **Nickname**, above).

Peterborough United

Peterborough United was formed in 1934 as a successor to the disbanded Peterborough and Fletton United club, which was itself founded in 1923 but suspended by the FA during the 1932–3 season. Peterborough Football Club was named after the Cambridgeshire city, which became known as a *Burg* or 'town' in the tenth century. 'Peter' records the dedication of the Benedictine abbey there to St Peter. The present cathedral was built in the twelfth century on the site of the former abbey.

Nickname: *The Posh*

There are various theories about when Peterborough acquired their nickname but it was almost certainly inherited from earlier, unconnected professional clubs in their home city.

One theory is that the name emerged when Pat Tirrel, player-manager of Fletton United, announced in the 1921 close season that he wanted to sign 'Posh players for a Posh team' to compete in the Northamptonshire League (later the United Counties League). Fletton, previously known as the 'Brickies' re-formed as Peterborough and Fletton United in 1923 (see above) and both nicknames were used throughout the 1920s. Supporters complained that 'Posh' references were sometimes used by newspapers in a derisory fashion.

Another suggestion is that when Peterborough played their first game on 1 September 1934 in their Midland League debut against Gainsborough Trinity as the successors to Peterborough and Fletton United, the team was greeted with cries of 'Up the Posh' by the crowd who admired their smart new kit. Since the last major Posh history was published in the early 1990s, the 'Posh new team' theory has become the favourite, as references have been found in newspapers that date back to well before the current club took over.

The word 'posh' is often said to date back to the days when wealthy passengers travelling by sea from England to India with P&O favoured a cabin on the port side on the outward voyage and on the starboard side on the way back ('Port Out, Starboard Home'), to avoid the worst of the sun. Passengers were booked POSH, and the word later became identified with anything exclusive or smart. This explanation is almost certainly untrue: P&O has no evidence of a single POSH booking. There was no difference in the cost of a cabin on the port or starboard side, and not much difference in the heat, either. The word may originate in a slang term meaning either money or a dandy.

Ground: *London Road Stadium*
Peterborough have been at *London Road* since their formation in 1934. The ground is named after London Road, which runs in front of the stadium and is the main route from the city towards London.

The stands are *Main, London Road Terrace, Moys End* (built on the site of Thomas Moy's old wagon works, linked to nearby Peterborough East Station) and the *Thomas Cook South Stand (Glebe Road)*.

Crest
The club badge is the same as the city's coat of arms, granted in 1960. It features a central shield with crossed keys, the symbol of St Peter, signifying the great monastery dating from about 650 around which the city developed. The Danes destroyed the monastery in 870 and its replacement burnt down in 1116, although the foundations can still be seen beneath the cathedral. Work began the following year on the present structure and was completed within the century. The two winged lions rampant on either side of the shield were adopted from the arms of the Lord Paramount of Peterborough and the first Earl of the town.

Fanzine: *The Peterborough Effect*
The fanzine is named after an advertising campaign launched in the 1980s to attract business to Peterborough.

Websites: *Posh Net* (www.posh.net), *Talking Posh* (http://peterboroughunited.rivals.net)
Posh Net and Talking Posh are references to the club's nickname (see **Nickname**, above).

Plymouth Argyle

The team was formed as the football section of the Argyle Athletic Club, a cricket and athletics club, in September 1886, at a meeting in a room above the Borough Arms Coffee Tavern in Bedford Street in the centre of Plymouth. The meeting was organised by F. Howard Grose and W. Pethybridge, ex-pupils of Dunheved College in Launceston, Cornwall, who wanted to start a new club with former public schoolboys. While working in Plymouth they shared rooms in the newly built Argyll Terrace, sometimes known as Argyle Terrace. The street in Mutley, now a northern district of Plymouth, dates back to the 1880s when the Argyll and Sutherland Highlanders were stationed in the city. During a discussion at the meeting about the name of the club, Grose suggested that the team should aim to play in the style of the Highlanders, whose teamwork in the Army Cup had impressed him. The club was thus named Argyle, a fashionable name at the time due to Queen Victoria's great interest in Scotland. 'Argyle' comes from the Gaelic *earraghaidheal*, meaning 'the boundary of the Gaels'.

On turning professional in 1903, the club added 'Plymouth' to its name, after the famous Devon city and port. 'Plymouth' means 'place at the mouth of the river Plym' and became the city's name in 1439. The name of the river itself comes from Plympton, now an eastern suburb, whose name means 'plum tree village'. Plymouth stands in a dramatic position at the mouths of the Plym and Tamar and at the head of Plymouth Sound, a natural basin of calm water hemmed in with islands and promontories.

Nickname: *The Pilgrims*
The nickname commemorates the Pilgrim Fathers who sailed from Plymouth in the *Mayflower* in 1620 to found the first colony in New England at New Plymouth, Massachusetts. The Pilgrims broke away from the Church of England because they wished to commit themselves to a life based on the Bible. One congregation from the village of Scrooby in Nottinghamshire emigrated to Amsterdam in 1608 to escape religious persecution and then moved to Leiden where they remained for almost twelve years. In 1617 the congregation voted to emigrate to America. The term 'Pilgrims' was first used to describe

these people.

A small ship, the *Speedwell*, carried the emigrants to Southampton where they were to join another group and pick up a second ship. They originally set sail in the *Speedwell* and *Mayflower* from Southampton on 5 August 1620 but had to put into Dartmouth when the *Mayflower* needed repair. Bad weather then drove them into Plymouth Sound where the *Speedwell* was abandoned. Following the delays and some disputes, the voyagers regrouped aboard the 180-ton *Mayflower* and 102 Pilgrims eventually sailed on 16 September. After sixty-five days they sighted Cape Cod and made their historic landing on the western side of Cape Cod Bay on 21 December. The main body of settlers followed on 26 December. They named their landing place Plymouth Harbour. The *Mayflower*'s passengers were first described as the Pilgrim Fathers in 1799.

Ground: *Home Park*

The club had no regular home ground until 1901 when they settled at *Home Park*, which was built originally for the Devonport Rugby Club and had staged rugby fixtures since 1894. The ground is named after the Home Farm which adjoined the present site.

The *Grandstand (Main Stand)* is the oldest of the stands, dating back to the 1940s. Behind the Main Stand are two training pitches, known as *Harper's Field* after a Scotland player who joined the club from Arsenal in the early 1930s and later served as a trainer and groundsman. The *Mayflower Stand* is a seated section of the Main Stand paddock named after the ship in which the Pilgrim Fathers sailed (see **Nickname**, above). The *Barn Park End* is named after one of the local farms that once surrounded the ground. The *Popular*, or *Lyndhurst, Side* is named after Lyndhurst Road, which is close to that side of the ground. It was called the Popular Side because it probably had the best view in the ground when it was terraced. The *Devonport End* is named after the nearby district of Devonport, which is renowned as a shipbuilding and naval base.

Crest

The badge shows the Mayflower (see **Nickname**, above) over a scroll with the club's initials, PAFC.

Fanzines: *Rub of the Greens, The Janners' Journal, The Guzzler, Hoof!, Way Out West, Evergreen*

When *Rub of the Greens* (www.rubofthegreens.com) started in 1990, as an Argyle fanzine it had to have the word 'green' in the title. The editors considered *Greenpeace* but were beaten to it by a fanzine that only ever had one issue, *The Green Piece*. They settled instead on *Rub of the Greens* because it was such a common phrase in football parlance, although at the time Plymouth never did seem to get the rub of the green. It was originally a golf, rather than football, term meaning a piece of good (or ill) fortune outside the competence of the player. Whenever the editor Stephen Nicholson hears a player, manager or commentator mention that someone did not get the rub of the green he sends them a copy.

The Janners' Journal, the Plymouth Argyle Cornish Supporters' Association bi-monthly newsletter, takes its name from 'Jan' the colloquial term for a West Countryman used particularly in the Royal Navy. *The Guzzler* was started and run by ex-servicemen who support Argyle and is so-called because 'Guz' is servicemen's slang for Devonport, or Plymouth (as Portsmouth is known as 'Pompey'). Guz is also short for 'Guzzle', relating to the West Country's love of cream teas. *Hoof!* was named after one of Plymouth's most popular players at the time, Mickey Heathcote, who was affectionately known as 'Hoof' because of the way he cleared his defensive lines. *Way Out West* got its name from the fact that Plymouth is the most westerly (and also most southerly) team in the League. *Evergreen* was after the team colours, because Argyle fans are For Ever Green.

Websites: *Semper Viridis* (www.semperviridis.co.uk),
***Greens on Screen* (www.greensonscreen.co.uk)**
Semper Viridis means 'Always Green' in Latin. Argyle have for many years run out to 'Semper Fidelis' (Always Faithful) by John Philip Sousa and the phrase has been adopted as an unofficial motto since the club do not have an official one. *Greens on Screen* was so-called as a reference to the team colours and because when it first started in 1999 the site showed clips of the goals from the local ITV station, which were therefore 'on screen'. It is also appropriate for a website on a PC screen.

Portsmouth

The club was formed as a limited company in 1898 by several local businessmen, including a brewer, Sir John Brickwood, in the High Street office of an Alderman and solicitor, J.E. Pink, after the city's leading club, Royal Artillery, had been suspended by the Football Association for breaching amateur regulations.

The name of the well-known port and naval base in Hampshire means 'place at the mouth of the port'.

Nicknames: *Pompey, Skates*

Pompey is the nickname of the city, as well as the club, and there are many theories as to how it originated. Some of these are listed in Mike Neasom's *Pompey – The History of Portsmouth Football Club* (Milestone Publications, 1984).

It may have originated with a group of Portsmouth-based sailors who scaled the 98-foot Pompey's Pillar near Alexandria in Egypt in 1781, and toasted their ascent in punch. Their feat earned them the Fleet's tribute as the Pompey boys. Alternatively, it could derive from *La Pompée*, an 80-gun French ship which was captured in 1793 and later fought with distinction in the battle of Algeciras in 1801, before becoming the guard ship to Portsmouth Harbour. Another suggestion is that the nickname can be traced to Portuguese sailors, who thought that the harbour looked like Bombay (Bom Bahia) because of its backdrop of hills: 'Bombay' became 'Pompey'. Another possible source can be found in 'Pom.P', a reference to Portsmouth Point, the entry made in the log by ships entering Portsmouth harbour. Navigational charts use this abbreviation. It could also have originated in a drunkard's slurred pronunciation of 'Portsmouth Point', where there were many taverns popular with sailors.

The nickname may be explained by the story of a drunken sailor who woke up during a lecture on the Roman Empire by Agnes Weston, the naval temperance worker, to hear her describe the murder of General Pompey. 'Poor old Pompey' he shouted. Another theory is that 'Pompey' derives from 'pompiers', the volunteer firemen who exercised on Southsea Common in the eighteenth century. Finally, it has been suggested that the pomp and ceremony associated with the Royal navy at Portsmouth gave rise to the nickname.

The nickname is recalled in the Pompey public house, now the club shop, which stands immediately outside the main entrance to the club's ground in Frogmore Road. The famous mock-Tudor pavilion, with a balcony overlooking the pitch, dates from 1905 when the ground was further developed.

'The Pompey Chimes' is the fans' song, delivered to the tune of a chiming clock: 'Play up Pompey, Pompey Play Up'. The origin of the song lies with the Royal Artillery (RA), who were the forerunners to Portsmouth FC (see above). The RA played many of their home games at the United Services ground in Burnaby Road, within earshot of the town hall clock. The referees at that time relied on the clock to let them know when it was four o'clock and the match should finish. At two or three minutes to four the crowd would chant the chimes of the hour to remind the referee to blow his whistle. The original tune of 'The Chimes' was slightly different to the modern version. The original words were:

> Play up Pompey.
> Just one more goal!
> Make tracks! What ho!
> Hallo! Hallo!

Portsmouth's link with chiming clocks may come from the city's shipyards or, alternatively, through confusion with the local name for Portsmouth's beaches, the Portsmouth Chines.

Skates is a derogatory term used by Southampton supporters to describe their south-coast rivals. It derives from the belief that Royal Navy sailors who were at sea for months on end would use the mouth of the skate fish to relieve their sexual frustrations.

Ground: *Fratton Park*

The ground near Fratton railway station, originally a market garden, was bought for £4,950 in 1898 by the local businessmen who established the club. *Fratton Park* is in the middle of Portsea Island, a narrow peninsular flanked by Langstone Harbour to the east and Portsmouth Harbour to the west. The ground is a few hundred yards east of Fratton Station on the line from Portsmouth to Waterloo. 'Fratton' is Old English for 'Froda's farm'.

The *Milton (Inter-City Cash) End* is named after the local district of Milton. In the north-east corner of the former terrace, where the floodlight pylon stands, was a section often called the 'Boilermakers' Hump', apparently once a favourite spot for local shipyard workers. *Fratton End (Ty Europe) Stand* is named after the railway station and sponsored by Ty Inc, an American toy company named after its founder Ty Warner. The two remaining stands are called *North* and *South*. The club is planning to build a new 35,000-seat stadium on the adjacent rail-freight depot site.

Crest

The traditional star and crescent motif in the team's colours above the club name is taken from the city's crest and signifies 'heaven's light is our guide'.

Fanzine: *January 3 '88*

January 3 '88 is named after the day Portsmouth beat their arch-rivals Southampton 2–0 at the Dell in a First Division (Premier League) game. Southampton dominated the match but could not score, whereas Pompey accomplished just two things in the whole game: scored twice.

Port Vale

The Stoke-on-Trent club takes its name from Port Vale House on Limekiln Road (now Scott Lidgett Road) in Longport, Burslem, where it was formed. The official date of Port Vale's formation is 1876, although a wealth of evidence suggests that 1879 is the probable date. The Vale in the name refers to the valley of Fowlea Brook, the Fowlea being one of the main upper tributaries of the River Trent. Burslem is situated on the valley's eastern ridge. Several landmarks in the Longport district adopted the name Port Vale, including Port Vale Street, which still exists, a canal wharf and a mill. The club added 'Burslem', one of the six towns of the Potteries, to its name in 1884 when it moved to a venue next to the station in the town. Port Vale became bankrupt in 1907 but was re-formed by local businessmen in 1913. They lured the club over the Burslem border to the Kent Street Old Recreation Ground in the heart of Hanley and the club then dropped Burslem from its name. Hanley is the centre of the region and the largest of its towns.

Nickname: *Valiants*
The nickname is a play on the club name.

Ground: *Vale Park*
In 1950 *Vale Park* became the club's sixth Staffordshire home, after the directors agreed to construct the finest stadium in the north with a capacity of 70,000. Work began in 1944 and was still far from complete when Port Vale moved in, with more stands and a stadium railway station to come. Unfortunately, the money ran out and it became clear that Vale's 'Wembley of the North' would remain a dream.

The stands are called *Railway/Paddock Stand, Hamil Road End, Lorne Street Stand* and *Bycars Road End*. The Railway End takes its name from Burslem Railway Station, which was on the far side of the present Co-op car park. It was part of a loop line closed in the late 1960s; no trace of it remains today.

Crest
The badge consists of a 'bottle oven', a coal- or wood-fired kiln

shaped like a bottle, and a Stafford Knot, the symbolic knot of Staffordshire. It also enshrines 1876 as the date of Port Vale's formation. From the eighteenth century until the 1960s bottle ovens were the dominating feature of the Staffordshire Potteries: there were over 2,000 of them in the region. Some small factories had only one bottle oven, while other large pot banks had as many as twenty-five.

The Stafford Knot, although not heraldic in its own right, is steeped in history. A popular romantic notion is that it was used in barbaric times by a Stafford County Sheriff, who invented it to hang three criminals at the same time, but the evidence clearly contradicts this idea. The earliest recording of the knot is the shaft of a stone cross in Stoke-on-Trent churchyard. The cross dates back to between AD 750 and 850, although the knot device could have been added at a later date. Lady Joan Stafford (later Lady Wake) used a seal with a border made up of her husband's badge, the Wake Knot, consisting of the initials W and O (for Wake and Ormond) intertwined. The seal, which is in the British Museum, depicts a cordon of four knots in the shape of the Stafford Knot. The knot was passed down through the Earl's family and was gradually adopted by the citizens and freemen of Stafford until it was eventually used in the Stafford Borough coat of arms. It is incorporated into the badges and symbols of many organisations and companies in the county, such as the Staffordshire police, fire and ambulance services.

Preston North End

Preston's origins can be traced back to a cricket and rugby club formed in 1863, which played most sports. The club adopted the name Preston North End in 1867 after moving to the newly laid out Moor Park, opposite their current ground at Deepdale (see **Ground**, below), simply because their new location was at the north end of the town. The club took up football in 1879 before focusing exclusively on the sport from 1881.

The Lancashire town near Manchester has a name found elsewhere in the country, meaning 'priests' village', from Old English *preosta-tun*. The name does not necessarily imply that priests lived there, but rather that the place was an endowment for priests who served a church somewhere else.

Motto
Princeps Pacis. Prince of Peace.

Nicknames: *The Lilywhites, North End*
Lilywhites is a reference to the team's white shirts, while *North End* comes from the club name.

Ground: *Deepdale*
The club settled at *Deepdale*, originally part of Deepdale Farm, in 1875.

The *Tom Finney (West) Stand* is named after the club's renowned England winger, known as the Preston Plumber, his trade when he joined Preston as an amateur in 1937. He made 433 League appearances between 1946 and 1959, scoring 187 goals – still a club record. Finney also scored thirty goals in seventy-six internationals between 1946 and 1958, and played in every position in the forward line. He was voted Footballer of the Year in 1954 and 1957, the first player to earn the accolade twice, and was awarded the OBE in 1961. The stand, which opened in March 1996, bears a picture of Finney, now the club president, picked out in white seating.

The *Bill Shankly (Fulwood End) Stand* is also known as the *Kop* (see **Liverpool**, Ground). Scottish-born Shankly was the celebrated manager under whose leadership Liverpool emerged as one of the greatest teams in English football history. However, before his managerial success, he had a successful playing career as a wing-half with Carlisle United and Preston, with whom he won an FA Cup winners' medal in 1938 in a 1–0 win over Huddersfield Town after extra time. He also won five caps for Scotland before he retired from playing in March 1949. One of Shankly's sayings became famous: 'Some people say football is a matter of life and death. They're wrong. It's much more important than that.' Shankly was awarded an OBE in 1974 and died on 29 September 1981.

The *Pavilion Stand (East Side)* was a 40-yard-long stand built to celebrate the club's promotion to the First Division (now Premier League) in 1934. With its lift, polished floors and suspended wooden panelling over the seats, it was designed to serve as the club's prestige headquarters. Planning permission has been granted for the construction of a new two-tier stand to replace the Pavilion Stand and take the ground's capacity to 30,000.

The *Alan Kelly Stand (Town End)* is named after the club's popular Ireland goalkeeper. Kelly began by playing for Drumcondra in 1954 before moving to Preston, where he stayed for the rest of his career. He had to wait until Fred Else moved to Blackburn Rovers before he got his chance but when it came he grabbed it with both hands, playing in 447 League games in thirteen years. He was in goal for the 1964 FA Cup final which Preston lost 3–2 to West Ham United. He won forty-seven caps for Ireland between 1956 and 1973, making his debut in a 3–0 win over the world champions, Germany. After retiring with a shoulder injury in 1973, aged 37, Kelly had a spell as the Ireland coach and assistant manager and also worked as a goalkeeping coach with Preston and Everton. He emigrated to the United States in 1985 where he became a coach for DC United in Washington. Kelly is the father of Alan Jnr (Sheffield United) and Gary (Oldham Athletic).

Crest

The club's coat of arms, adopted in 1933 depicts the lamb of St Wilfred kneeling above the club name. Preston North End FC replaced the initials PP, which actually stand for *Princeps Pacis*, 'Prince of Peace' (see **Motto**, above), though some suggest the initials actually mean 'Proud Preston', a reference to the club and the town, which is the administrative centre of Lancashire and has always been important because of its strategic position on the River Ribble astride the lowland route from Scotland.

Websites: *Lilywhite Magic* (**www.lilywhites.net**), *Who's That Jumping Off The Pier* (**http://prestonnorthend.rivals.net**)

Lilywhite Magic is a reference to the club nickname and the sort of form the players occasionally conjure up on the pitch. 'Who's that jumping off the pier' is a line from a popular Preston terrace song about the club's rivals Blackpool and their inability to beat North End. Blackpool has three cast-iron nineteenth-century piers on the so-called Golden Mile. The North Pier, the first to be opened in 1863, is now a listed building.

Queen's Park Rangers

The club was probably formed in 1886 through the amalgamation of two west London teams, Christchurch Rangers and St Jude's Institute FC (formed 1882). The new club was originaly called St Jude's, but as most of the players came from the Queen's Park district of north-west London, this name was adopted a year later. As is the case with many parks in England, the name honours Queen Victoria. There is still a park of that name today, although QPR have never played there.

Nicknames: *Rangers, R's*
Both nicknames are taken from the third part of the club name.

Ground name: *Loftus Road*
The club settled in 1917 two miles south-west of Queen's Park at the former home of Shepherd's Bush FC, an amateur club that had disbanded during the First World War. It is officially called the *Rangers Stadium* but has always been known as *Loftus Road*, after the highway on which one end of the ground is situated. QPR have played at twelve grounds – more than any other League club.

The *South Africa Road Stand* is named after one of the roads near the ground which were themselves named in honour of Common-wealth countries competing at the 1908 Olympic Games in London. The athletes' village was close to Loftus Road. White City, where QPR have also played, was the world's first purpose-built Olympic stadium when it was built for the Games. (Incidentally, White City got its nickname because so many of the pavilions were white.) The *Alfred McAlpine Homes (Main) Stand* is known as the *Ellerslie Road Stand*, but is now sponsored by the construction company Alfred McAlpine.

The *School End* is named after Ellerslie Road School, which has since been replaced by flats. The school's most famous ex-student is Jim Gregory, who was QPR chairman from the 1960s to the 1980s. As a schoolboy, he used to stand on the wall around the school to look out over the Loftus Road ground. Gregory took over when the team was in the Third Division (South) and transformed the club into a First Division (top flight) outfit with signings like Stan Bowles and Rodney Marsh. The *Loftus Road End* is known as the *Loft* to regulars.

Crest
The current crest dates from 1982, the year recognised by the club as its centenary year. It was also the year in which QPR reached the FA Cup final for the first and only time, losing 1–0 to Tottenham Hotspur after a replay. A simple crest showing the initials QPR over-laid with a football had been adopted in the 1970s: it was upgraded to a design of 'QPR' in ornamental type, circled and with a scroll underneath including the words 'Loftus Road', below the date 1882.

Fanzines: *In the Loft, A Kick Up the Rs*
In the Loft (http://www.qpr-mad.co.uk) is a reference to the Loftus Road End, known as the Loft (see **Ground,** above). *A Kick Up the Rs* is a pun, playing on the team's nickname and the slang word for posterior.

Reading

The club was formed in 1871 at a meeting at the Bridge Street Rooms in the Berkshire town. It is the oldest League club south of Nottingham. It amalgamated with the Reading Hornets in 1877 and was then joined by Earley FC in 1889.

Reading means 'place of Read's people', *read* being an Anglo-Saxon word meaning 'red one'.

Nickname: *The Royals*

The nickname is a reference to the club's location in the county town of 'Royal Berkshire', a title made official with a grant in the 1930s.

Reading's original nickname was the *Biscuitmen* because Huntley & Palmers were one of the major employers in the town. The biscuit factory occupied a huge site to the east of the town centre close to Reading's old ground at Elm Park. Huntley & Palmers sports' ground was directly opposite Elm Park on the former site of the Berkshire County Cricket Ground. By the early 1970s, however, the company had been taken over and the factory closed. Nobody in the town used the Biscuitmen name any longer, although it still occasionally surfaced in the national press.

It was left to the supporters' club to rectify the situation. During the 1976 close season, they organised a competition with the *Reading Chronicle* to find a new nickname. In the middle of June, the team's manager Charlie Hurley selected *The Royals* as the winning entry. This name had been put forward by eleven people, so their names were all put into a hat and Hurley drew out Mr B. Palmer of Linden Road as the winner. The launch of the new nickname was a low key affair, and it took some time to become established before eventually the chant of 'Come on you Royals' was regularly heard during matches. 'I like The Royals,' says the *Farewell to Elm Park* website (www.elmpark.com). 'It fits the nature of our club – homely, respectable, and with occasional delusions of grandeur.'

Ground: *Madejski Stadium*

The ground is named after the club chairman, John Madejski, a multi-millionaire auto magazine publisher who bought Robert Maxwell's stake in Reading in September 1990. Madejski, whose name appears in many places in Reading, from the art gallery to a hotel, made his money from *Auto Trader* magazine, which he sold to Hearst Publishing for £174 million in 1998.

'I was led to believe that the club would go under if I did not step in,' said Madejski, describing himself as 'just a supporter' who felt he could give the nondescript town an identity:

> I consider Reading as where I'm from. Having lived in California and travelled the world, I know what it's like to find a newspaper in a far-flung place and see the football results. Just to see the name of Reading in print, it's a reminder, it's like a suck of the thumb. Reading has never been much of anything; it's too close to London for that. If you want to do something for the town, you can help the hospital – but the football club really touches a lot of people. I did not want Reading to lose its football club in my generation.

Madejski was born on 28 April 1941 in Stoke-on-Trent, but his family moved to Reading when he was seven. He became a biscuit salesman for manufacturers Huntley and Palmer in the late 1950s (see **Nickname**, above) and then travelled to California, where he worked on a ranch and as a car salesman. He returned to Britain in 1966 and three years later joined the *Reading Evening Post* as a classified advertising sales executive. While he was on holiday in Florida in the mid-1970s he saw a car sales magazine that included photographs of the vehicles for sale, and immediately realised the potential of the idea. Along with a colleague, Madejski founded *Thames Valley Trader* in 1976, based on a model he had seen in the United States. Initially the magazine sold everything from houses to cars and even aircraft, but in 1977 he split the cars from the homes and founded *Thames Valley Auto Trader*. In 1978, the magazine became national. The company, still based in Reading, employs more than 1,000 people. In 2004 Madejski was among the top 200 wealthiest people in the UK on the *Sunday Times* Rich List, with a net worth in the region of £305 million. He was awarded the OBE in 2000 in 'recognition of his contribution to Reading Football Club and the Reading Community'.

The stadium was built at a cost of £37 million on a formerly contaminated rubbish tip surrounded by methane vents. The opening match was against Luton Town on 22 August 1998. Before the opening of the new stadium, the club had played at *Elm Park* for 102 years. The stands are called *North, South, East* and *West*.

Crest

The crown on the crest refers to the club's location in the Royal County of Berkshire, and is a symbol of the town's royal connections as the burial place of Henry I and the recipient of various royal charters. The lion represents the statue, designed by George Blackall Simonds, that stands in Forbury Gardens in the centre of Reading. The Forbury, or Maiwand, Lion, the most important public sculpture in Reading, commemorates the lives lost by the Royal Berkshire regiment in Afghanistan in about 1880. (The club mascot is Kingsley the Lion.) The blue and white hoops reflect the club's traditional kit, worn for their first game in 1872 and reintroduced in 1938, since when it has been regularly used, albeit with some interruptions. The badge was designed by Cream Design, a local company whose employees are nearly all Reading season ticket holders. It was introduced in August 1998 to coincide with the move from Elm Park to the Madejski Stadium.

Fanzines: *The Whiff, Junction 11, Elm Park Disease, Taking the Biscuit*

The Whiff was named after the so-called 'Whitley whiff' associated with the Whitley sewage works near the new stadium. *Junction 11* takes its name from the M4 motorway exit for the Madejski Stadium. *Elm Park Disease* refers to the club's old ground. *Taking the Biscuit* comes from the team's former nickname, the Biscuitmen (see **Nickname**, above) in 1974.

Websites: *Hob Nob Anyone?* (www.royals.org), *Off At Eleven* (http://reading.rivals.net), *1871 Royals* (www.sportnetwork.net/main/s253.htm)

Hob Nob Anyone? is a reference to Hob Nob biscuits, associated with the club's former Biscuitmen nickname (see **Nickname**, above) and because it enables fans to hob nob, or socialise, with each other. The expression comes from an old phrase 'hob or nob', meaning to drink to one another by turns. *Off At Eleven* is named, like the *Junction 11* fanzine, after the M4 motorway exit for the Madejski Stadium. 1871 Royals refers to the year the club was formed, and its nickname (see **Nickname**, above).

Rochdale

Rochdale Town was founded in 1900 but went out of existence in 1907. A new club, Rochdale AFC, was immediately formed, largely due to the efforts of Harvey Rigg, the former secretary of the St Clements Rugby Club, which had also folded. He needed a team to help pay the rent at their St Clements ground.

The name of the town at the edge of the Pennines near Manchester originated as something like 'Rachedham' from Old English *raeced* (building or hall) and *ham* (homestead), so it was a 'homestead with a hall'. The name Rached passed to the river, and later the river valley became known as the Rached-dale, which eventually became Rochdale and the River Roch.

Motto
Crede Signo. The sign of trust and confidence.

Nickname: *The Dale*
The nickname is taken from the club's name.

Ground: *Spotland Stadium*
Spotland is named after the area in which the ground is situated. Spotland was a township that became part of Rochdale Borough in 1856.

The stands are the *Pearl Street End (WMG*, after the sponsors, a local firm of accountants, Wyatt, Morris and Golland), *Main Stand (Motorama), Willbutts Lane End (Westrose Leisure Stand)* and *Sandy Lane End (Thwaites Beer)*.

Crest
The crest is a variant of the arms of the former County Borough of Rochdale granted by Heralds' College in 1857. At its centre a shield includes a sack of wool and a cotton plant, representing local industries. Around the edge of the shield sit eight birds (known as martlets, swifts or house-martins). These are taken from the Rachdale family coat of arms on which the Borough's arms are based. A fleece and the iron centre of an old mill-stone, known as a mill-rind, are above the shield while the club motto (see **Motto**, above) is included in a

scroll below the shield. The club's name and nickname are included in a ring around the arms, with Rochdale AFC at the top and The Dale at the bottom.

Fanzines: *The Dale Blues*
The Dale Blues is taken from the nickname and the club's colours, allied to the feelings of the fans when the team is not playing well.

Rotherham United

Rotherham was formed in 1870, before becoming Rotherham Town in the late 1880s. Another club, Thornhill United, was founded in 1877 and changed its name to Rotherham County in 1905. In 1925, Town merged with Rotherham County to form Rotherham United.

The town near Sheffield takes its name from the River Rother, with *ham* meaning 'homestead'. The river's name is probably of Celtic origin meaning 'main river'.

Nickname: *The Merry Millers*
The nickname is a reference to the town's many mills including a large windmill that was near the ground. There is still a Hovis flour mill nearby.

Ground: *Millmoor Ground*
Rotherham moved to *Millmoor*, named after nearby Millmoor Lane, in 1907. The area is surrounded by mills and moors, hence the name.

The *Railway End* is so-called because the ground once belonged to Midland Railway, whose line ran nearby. The *Tivoli End* is named after the Tivoli Cinema, on the other side of the road on Masborough Street. Built just before the First World War, it was a magnificent example of early cinema architecture. It has been replaced by a car park but the social club behind preserves the Tivoli name. The *Millmoor Lane Community Stand* is named after nearby Millmoor Lane.

Crest
The badge shows a windmill above a football, a reference to the many mills in the area (see **Nickname**, above).

Fanzine: *Moulin Rouge*
Moulin Rouge takes its name from the famous music hall whose name means 'red mill'. The name is appropriate for a team that plays in red, on a ground with a mill nearby.

Websites: *Millers Net* (**www.millersnet.co.uk**), *Millers Mad* (**www.rotherhamunited-mad.co.uk**)
Millers Net and *Millers Mad* are references to the club's nickname.

Rushden and Diamonds

Rushden Town was founded in 1889 although the present club only emerged in 1992. A merger with another Northamptonshire club, Irthlingborough Diamonds (formed in 1946), was engineered by a local multi-millionaire, Max Griggs, owner of the local Dr Marten's footwear company. He bought the two non-League clubs and amalgamated them.

The name 'Rushden' comes from Old English *risdene* meaning 'a valley where rushes grow'. 'Diamonds' evolved from 'Dynamo'. When Cyril Jones founded the Irthlingborough club as a youth team, he named them after the top European team at the time, the mighty Moscow Dynamo. In 1945 Dynamo had been the first Soviet team to tour Britain after the end of the Second World War. They played four games, drawing 3–3 with Chelsea, beating Arsenal 4–3, crushing Cardiff City 10–1 and drawing 2–2 with Rangers in Glasgow.

Nicknames: *The Russians, The Diamonds*
Russians is a variation of 'Rushden' and 'Diamonds' taken directly from the team name and a reference to the nationality of Moscow Dynamo, after whom the club is named (see above). *The Diamonds* is from the team name..

Ground: *Nene Park*
Irthlingborough Diamonds originally acquired *Nene Park* from the local water board in 1969. The ground is named after the River Nene, which flows nearby and itself has an ancient Celtic or pre-Celtic name.

The stands are named *North, South, East Terrace (AirWair Stand,* after the brand name of Dr Marten's) and *Peter De Banke Terrace (West),* which was opened in 1994 in memory of the former Rushden Town and Irthlingborough Diamonds player.

Crest
The crest incorporates the insignia of the two former clubs, Rushden Town and Irthlingborough Diamonds, which make up Rushden and Diamonds. The badge features a shield divided into four quarters.

From Rushden Town comes a rampant lion in the top left-hand quarter. It was taken from the crest of the Sartoris family who in 1922 donated a piece of land on Hayden Road to the Rushden Sports Club that became home to Rushden Town, as were and the red and white hoops that adorn the bottom right-hand quarter of the crest. The cross-keys in the top right-hand quarter of the crest, representing the keys to heaven and hell, were taken from St Peter's Church in Irthlingborough, while the blue diamonds in the bottom left-hand quarter were also on Irthlingborough Diamonds original badge. The crest has a wavy line representing the River Nene, which runs close to the club's Nene Park ground. The nearby bridge over the river also features the cross-keys from the church.

Fanzine: *Rushin and Rantin*
The fanzine's title incorporates a variation on the team's name and the right of fans to complain.

Scunthorpe United

The club traces its history back to 1899 when Brumby Hall FC (formed about 1895) merged with a number of other clubs and changed its name to Scunthorpe United. In 1910 the club amalgamated with North Lindsey United to become Scunthorpe and Lindsey United. The 'and Lindsey' was dropped in 1958.

The Humberside town has a Danish name from its location inside the Danelaw, a part of north and east England occupied by the Danes from the ninth to the eleventh century. Scunthorpe means 'Skuma's farm' with the Scandinavian personal name followed by Old Norse *thor*, a term for an outlying farm that relies on a larger one.

Nickname: *The Iron*

The nickname is a reference to the town's history as a centre of iron and steel manufacturing. Scunthorpe gained its size and importance through the iron-ore deposits discovered there in the 1870s. However, by the start of the millennium there was just one steelworks left, evidence of a decline in a proud tradition.

Ground: *Glanford Park*

The club moved to the £2.1 million stadium in 1988. It is named after Scunthorpe's neighbouring town, where it is situated and which also agreed a £200,000 ten-year sponsorship deal with the club.

The stands are called *Main (Grove Wharf East)*, *Scunthorpe Telegraph Family Stand (West)*, *NLC Study United FC* (formerly the *Don Cass Community Stand*) and *South*. The NLC Study United FC stand is sponsored by North Lincolnshire Council to publicise the learning centre based at the ground. This joint project between the council and the club aims to use football as a way of raising standards of literacy and numercy among children.

Crest

The hand holding an iron girder in the club's claret and blue colours represents unity and strength of purpose, as befits a club in an iron and steel town.

Websites: *Iron-Bru Net* (www.scunthorpeunited-mad.co.uk),
Iron Online (http://scunthorpeunited.rivals.net)
Iron Bru is a reference to the team's nickname the Iron and also to
Irn-Bru, a popular mild citrus drink with caffeine. It was a printed
fanzine but is now only available online. *Iron Online,* previously
called *Any Old Iron,* is a reference to the club nickname (see
Nickname, above) based on the title of a song written by Chas
Collins, E.A. Sheppard and Fred Terry and sung by the Cockney
music hall entertainer Harry Champion. Champion (real name
William Crump) was born in Shoreditch, London in 1866 and first
appeared in music hall at the age of 15. In 1888 he changed his stage
name from Will Conray and, with a wide repertoire of songs, many
of them sung at breakneck speed, became one of music hall's most
successful artists. He continued working into his seventies and died
in London in January 1942. The title of the song refers to scrap
metal merchants, who used to go round the streets with a horse and
cart calling their trade, 'Old Iron' or 'Rag and Bones', and buying
junk for what we now call recycling:

> Any old iron, any old iron,
> Any any any old iron?
> You look neat, talk about a treat!
> You look so dapper from your napper to your feet.
> Dressed in style, brand-new tile,
> And your father's old green tie on.
> But I wouldn't give you tuppence for your old watch and chain,
> Old iron, old iron.

Sheffield United

Sheffield United grew out of Sheffield Cricket Club, formed in 1854. Its members began to play football a year later as Sheffield Football Club, making them the oldest football club in the world, but they did not form a permanent team until September 1889 when the Ground Committee at Bramall Lane formed Sheffield United in order to make better use of the venue's facilities and generate additional income.

The club takes its name from the South Yorkshire city, the largest in Yorkshire and the fourth largest in England, although the county's second city after Leeds. 'United' refers to the union of the cricket and football teams.

Sheffield stands at the foot of the Derbyshire hills where the River Sheaf meets the River Don. Its name means 'open land by the Sheaf', the small river that flows through the town before entering the larger Don. 'Sheaf' means 'dividing one', from Old English *sceath*, 'sheath', because the river formed the boundary between Derbyshire and the former West Riding of Yorkshire. The second part of the name comes from Old English *feld*, which gives modern English 'field' but originally described an extensive region of open land, as in South Africa's veld.

Nickname: *The Blades*
The nickname is a reference to the city's long history of manufacturing steel, which Sheffield has specialised in since the eighteenth century. It was also formerly the nickname of the city's other major club, Sheffield Wednesday. United were once known as *The Cutlers*: the city has been a centre for producing cutlery since the Middle Ages. Technological advances in steel production later turned Sheffield into one of the country's foremost centres of heavy and specialist engineering.

Ground: *Bramall Lane*
The ground, first laid out in 1854, was originally the home of Sheffield Cricket Club. Until 1973 the football pitch overlapped the cricket pitch by 20 yards. Sheffield FC was the first club to play football at *Bramall Lane*, in December 1862. The ground was regularly

used by The Wednesday, later Sheffield Wednesday, from 1868 until 1887. On 14 October 1878 it became the first venue in the world to stage a game under floodlights.

The *South (Global Windows) Stand* is named after a local company. The *John Street (HFS Loans) Stand* is named after the nearby street. The *Bramall Lane (Gordon Lamb) Stand* is named after the nearby lane from which the ground also takes its name. The *Kop (Hallam FM) Stand* is named after the sponsors, Hallam FM, one of the leading radio stations in South Yorkshire and the North Midlands (see also **Liverpool**, Ground).

Crest

The circular badge shows two crossed cutlasses, a reference to the club's nickname, The Blades, and the Yorkshire rose, a symbol of the county. The words 'Sheffield United' and '1889', the date of the club's formation, surround the swords and rose.

Websites: *Greasy Chip Buttie* (www.greasychipbuttie.co.uk), *Gallon of Magnet* (www.gallonofmagnet.cjb.net), *Blades Online* (http://sheffieldunited.rivals.net), *Red and White Wizards* (www.redandwhite-wizards.co.uk), *Bladesmen* (www.bladesmen.co.uk), *Blades Mad* (www.sheffieldunited-mad.co.uk)

Greasy Chip Buttie is named after a terrace song that originated in the late 1970s. The words celebrate the many pleasures that can be had in Sheffield, culminating in the target of the fan's adoration, Sheffield United. It is the club's unofficial anthem sung to the tune of John Denver's 'Annie's Song', a UK number one hit in 1974. 'Butties', available in many of the local fish and chip shops, consist of chips, ideally greasy and sprinkled with salt and vinegar, inside a white sandwich roll or bap. *Gallon of Magnet* takes its title from a line in the 'Greasy Chip Buttie' song and refers to Magnet beer, which is brewed near Sheffield:

> You fill up my senses
> Like a gallon of Magnet
> Like a packet of Woodbines
> Like a good pinch of snuff
> Like a night out in Sheffield
> Like a greasy chip buttie
> Like Sheffield United

Come thrill me again...
Na Na Na Na Na Na Na...

Woodbine cigarettes used to be popular in Sheffield, while snuff is another local delicacy.

Blades Online refers to the club's nickname (see **Nickname,** above). The site is also home to the *Flashing Blade* fanzine. *The Red and White Wizards* is what the team have long been known as among their supporters. *Bladesmen* and *Blades Mad* also refer to the nickname.

Sheffield Wednesday

The football club was formed on Wednesday 4 September 1867 at a meeting in the Adelphi Hotel by members of the Sheffield Wednesday Cricket Club, to keep the cricket team together during the winter months. The cricket club had started in 1816 and was so called because its members met and played on Wednesday afternoons, the traditional weekly half-day closing in Sheffield, which provided a holiday for the workers to play sport. The team severed its links with the cricketers in 1883. It was known to fans simply as The Wednesday until 1929 when many believe the city name was added under the team's manager, Bob Brown. However, the club was known as Sheffield Wednesday as far back as 1883 when its former ground at Olive Grove had the name painted on the stand roof. 'Sheffield Wednesday' was also inscribed on the FA Cup when Wednesday won it in 1896 and 1907.

(See **Sheffield United** for the origins of the city name.)

Motto
Consilio et Animis. Intelligence and Courage.

Nicknames: *The Owls*, *Wednesday*
The Owls refers to Owlerton, the original name of the club's Hillsborough ground (see **Ground**, below). The nickname, which can be traced as far back as 1907, is somewhat artificial since the ground's old name was generally pronounced 'Olerton'. Wednesday's original nickname was *The Blades*, now used by their city rivals United. It was used until the early part of the nineteenth century when a player presented them with an owl mascot to honour their stadium at Owlerton, since when the club has been known as The Owls.

Ground: *Hillsborough*
The club played at *Bramall Lane* for the first twenty years but eventually settled at Owlerton in 1899 – a bold decision since it was then outside the city to the north-west of Sheffield in a sparsely populated area with poor public transport links. The land had belonged to James Dixon, a wealthy silversmith who in 1892 had handed over his home, Hillsborough Hall and its grounds, to the Corporation. In

1914, when the name of the parliamentary constituency in which it lies was changed, the *Owlerton Stadium* was renamed *Hillsborough*. By that time the Owlerton ground had already become known as Hillsborough among the supporters. Renaming the stadium after the suburb ensured they caught the right tram to the ground.

The stands are called *North (Sheffield Assay Office)*; *South (Appleby)*; *Spion (Hallam FM) Kop (Penistone Road End)*, named the Kop because it is built into a natural hill at the east end of the ground (see also **Liverpool**, Ground); and *West (Leppings Lane End*, after the nearby lane).

Crest

The district of Owlerton not only gave the club its nickname, it also provided the inspiration for the design of the crest. The simple line-drawn owl design has been used since 1995 and shows the familiar modern image of an owl sitting on the abbreviation of the club's name 'SWFC'. The crest is often displayed with the full club name below it.

Fanzines: *Spitting Feathers, The Blue and White Wizards, Out of the Blue, War of the Monster Trucks*

Spitting Feathers is an old expression meaning 'venting one's spleen', which is what fanzines do. The feathers relate to the Owls. *The Blue and White Wizards* is what the team have long been known as by supporters. *Out of the Blue* was originally going to be called *Into the Blue*, in other words 'into Wednesday' to reflect the enthusiasm of the fanzine writers but, as the editor Trevor Braithwait recalls, it 'just came to me one day when I was thinking of a name for the mag... it was almost out of the blue! I thought *Out of the Blue*, being an old adage, was more memorable.' *War of the Monster Trucks* took its name from a Yorkshire Television programme aired as Wednesday were celebrating their 1991 League Cup final victory over Manchester United. Much to the annoyance of Wednesday supporters, the team's celebrations were shown live on every regional station except Yorkshire.

Websites: *Owls Online* (http://sheffieldwednesday.rivals.net), *Owls Mad* (www.sheffieldwednesday-mad.co.uk)

Owls Online and *Owls Mad* are references to the club's nickname (see **Nicknames**, above).

Shrewsbury Town

Shrewsbury School, the boys' public school founded in 1552, provided a number of the early England and Wales internationals so it was not surprising that there was a Town club as early as 1876. However, the present Shrewsbury Town was formed in 1886.

The medieval county town of Shropshire has a name that means 'fortified place of the scrubland region' from Old English *scrubb* and *burh* (fortified place). The present spelling may have developed by association with 'shrew', which was formerly pronounced to rhyme with 'show'.

Nicknames: *Shrews, Town, Blues, Salop*
Shrews and *Town* come from the club's name, while *Blues* is a reference to the colour of the team's kit. *Salop* is from the Latin word for 'Shropshire', the county of western England bordering Wales. Since Shrewsbury is the only club in Shropshire 'Come on Salop' is often heard. 'Salopian' is still used for Shropshire people and boys from Shrewsbury School.

Ground: *Gay Meadow*
The club settled in 1910 at *Gay Meadow*, a well-used and much-loved venue that had been a favourite spot for people to have fun and play games for centuries. It was pleasantly situated on the banks of the River Severn, and overlooked by the town with its castle. The only change had been the construction of a railway embankment along the eastern side of the meadow carrying the line from mid-Wales and Hereford to Shrewsbury station.

The *Main Stand* incorporates the *Wakeman Stand*, the *Centre Stand* and the *Station Stand*. The *Riverside Terrace* is a reference to the River Severn that runs behind the ground. The southern terrace (the *Wakeman End*), like the Wakeman Stand, was named after the nearby Wakeman Technical School which was built between 1936 and 1938 on the site of the old Merevale House. The school's windows look down on to the ground. The *Station End* is a reference to Shrewsbury Station, which spans the river.

The club is planning to move to a new £10 million, 10,000 seater stadium at Oteley Road on the outskirts of town, near Moele Brace by the A5. It will be known as the *New Meadow* to preserve the links with Gay Meadow.

Crest
Shrewsbury and Atcham Borough Council's 'three loggerheads' coat of arms was used by the club from its formation until the early 1980s, when a more modern crest showing a shrew, after Town's nickname, was introduced. The town coat of arms was re-introduced as the club badge in 1992. *Floreat Salopia*, 'Flourish Shropshire' in Latin, also features on the county crest which is very similar to the town's coat of arms.

Fanzines: *The Mighty Shrew, Blue and Amber, A Large Scotch*
The Mighty Shrew (www.themightyshrew.co.uk) comes from the club's nickname (see **Nicknames**, above). *Blue and Amber* (http://shrewsburytown.rivals.net) is taken from the colour of the team's shirts. *A Large Scotch* (now a four-page pullout in each issue of *Blue and Amber*) refers to the large number of Scottish players the club had in the 1980s and their ability to drink large amounts of alcohol.

Website: *News of the Shrews* (http://mysite.wanadoo-members.co.uk/shrews2
News of the Shrews is a play on *News of the Screws*, a slang name for the *News of the World* newspaper, notorious for the number of stories it contains about sex. The editor of *News of the Shrews*, Richard Staines, a journalist, has explained 'I wanted to create a spoof tabloid site about my favourite football team, hence the girls in Shrewsbury tops.'

Southampton

Southampton was formed largely by players from the Deanery FC, which was established by school teachers in 1880. Most of the founders were connected with the young men's association (YMCA) of St Mary's Church, the mother church of Southampton in St Mary's Street. At the inaugural meeting in November 1885 the club was named Southampton St Mary's and the church's curate was elected president. 'St Mary's' was dropped from the name in 1897.

The city and port on the English channel has a name meaning 'southern Hampton' in contrast to 'northern Hampton', the present day Northampton. The towns were linked by a north–south route in medieval times. Southampton's 'hampton' is a 'waterside farm' or estate on a promontory (headland) from Old English *hamm* and *tun*. (The location of Southampton between the rivers Itchen and Test confirms this origin.) Northampton is a 'home farm' from *ham*. Both places were originally known as Hampton (see **Northampton**).

Nicknames: *The Saints, Scummers*
The *Saints* comes from the club's original name, Southampton Saint Mary's. *Scummers* is a derogatory name used by Portsmouth fans to describe their bitter south-coast rivals. There are a number of theories behind the name. It may have originated because Portsmouth, a Royal Navy dock, looks down on Southampton, a commercial port. Another possible explanation may lie in the word 'scum', naval slang for merchant seamen, a reference to scum floating on the water.

The most popular theory is that Scummers stands for 'Southampton Company of Union Men' (SCUM) and arose after a dispute between a local fishing company and its employees over wages, just before the First World War. The company had two branches, one in Portsmouth and the other in Southampton. The dispute escalated and eventually the union called a strike, which was solid among the Portsmouth Company Union Men and the Southampton dockers. Nothing was resolved, however, and after some weeks the strike was broken by the SCUM, ensuring the collapse of the dispute without any gain for the employees of either company. Not surprisingly, the Portsmouth dockers were so incensed that Scum or Scummer became a term of abuse for anyone from Southampton. However, there are serious doubts about this theory, since until the 1980s the commercial port in Portsmouth was very small, hardly more than a quayside, and dockers from Southampton are unlikely to have gained access to a Royal Navy establishment. The most likely story is that the nickname comes from the general use of the word as a term of abuse among fans everywhere.

Ground: *The Friends' Provident St Mary's Stadium*
The ground is named after St Mary's Church in St Mary's Street which gave the club its original name (see above). The ground is only about 500 yards from the church on the boundary of districts called Chapel and Northam but the whole area, including the heart of St Mary's, was devastated by bombing in the Second World War and their distinct identities became somewhat blurred as communities were displaced. The club is sponsored by the life assurance company Friends' Provident.

The stands are named after areas of the city close to the stadium. The *Chapel (South) Stand* is named after the chapel of St Mary's church. The *Kingsland (West)* and *Northam (North)* stands are named after the local districts. *Northam* is an Old English word for 'north hemmed-in land'. The land in the area is hemmed in by the last bend in the River Itchen before it reaches Southampton Water. The *Itchen Stand* is named after the nearby river.

Crest
The club's badge was designed by the fans in the 1970s and shows a red and white scarf topped by a black and white football with a gold halo. This rests on the main emblem, which includes a white Hampshire rose beneath the gently lapping tides of the Solent. Above this stands a tree, representing the nearby New Forest, which occupies the south-west corner of Hampshire between Southampton Water and the River Avon. The forest existed as such in 1016 but William the Conqueror formally established it as a game reserve around 1079 and gave it its name. 'Forest' was a legal term implying an area subject not to common law but to the forest law, designed to safeguard wild deer for the king's hunting. Today the forest covers some 144 square miles, attracting about 8 million visitors a year.

Fanzine: *Beautiful South*
The fanzine is named after the northern pop group who called them-
selves The Beautiful South as an ironic comment on southern
England. The fanzine used the name as a further irony.

Websites: *The Ugly Inside* (http://southampton.rivals.net),
Waterloo Sunset (www.londonsaints.com), *Up the Saints*
(www.upthesaints.com), *Saints World* (www.saintsworld.net),
Saints Forever (www.saintsforever.com)
The Ugly Inside is named after the two groups of fans, 'The Ugly
Men' (1990s) and 'The Inside Crew' (1980s), who got together to
produce a fanzine. *Waterloo Sunset* is a website and newsletter
produced by a club in London that has supported Southampton
since 1978. The title was suggested by a committee member because
his neighbours included members of The Kinks, who had had a hit
song of that name. It also recalled the sunsets he had seen over the
years as he travelled to Southampton from Waterloo Station with
the rest of the fans. The other websites all refer to the club's nickname (see **Nicknames**, above).

Southend United

The club was founded in 1906 as a rival to the longer established amateur club Southend Athletic. Southend United was named after the Essex resort on the Thames Estuary at the south end of Prittlewell, which is now a district of Southend. The town developed as recently as the nineteenth century after the Prince Regent decided in 1809 that the village of Prittlewell would provide a healthier climate than London for his wife Princess Caroline. She lodged at Prittlewell's 'south end', which then became the town's official name.

Nicknames: *The Shrimpers, The Blues*
The Shrimpers is a reference to the club's seaside location at Southend-on-Sea, where day-trippers and holiday makers enjoy the local seafood. *The Blues* comes from the colour of the team's strip.

Ground: *Roots Hall*
The club was based at *Roots Hall* when it was founded and moved back there in 1955. The ground was laid out in 1900 in the grounds of an eighteenth-century house called Roots Hall. The first club to play there was Southend Athletic, who made way for the newly formed United in 1906.

C2C West Stand is named after the sponsors, who run the Fenchurch Street to Shoeburyness railway line, formerly LTS (London-Tilbury-Southend) and now Coast2City. The *Online Financial (East) Stand* is named after the sponsors. The *Frank Walton (HiTec South) Stand* is named after Frank Walton, who performed almost every role at the club, as a player, coach, groundsman, director and chairman. The *Universal Cycle (North Bank) Stand* is named after the sponsors, a local firm with a director on the club's board.

Crest
The current badge, the fourth in the club's history, was introduced in 2002. The shrimp and the football replaced the anchor and lion that had previously appeared on the crest. The cutlasses are depicted on the coat of arms of Essex, granted on 15 July 1932. The arms,

attributed to the ancient kingdom of the East Saxons, were regarded as county arms long before the official grant. The cutlasses are distinctively notched sea axes, a reference to the word 'Saxon'.

Websites: *Shrimperzone* (www.shrimperzone.com),
Shrimpers.net (http://southendunited.rivals.net),
The Shrimpers Online (www.theshrimpers-online.co.uk),
Artful Shrimper (www.wenborn.freeserve.co.uk)
The website names all refer to the club's nicknames (see **Nicknames**, above).

Stockport County

Stockport County was formed at a meeting held by members of Wycliffe Congregational Chapel on Wellington Road South, in 1883. The club was originally called Heaton Norris Rovers, after its first home ground. Heaton Norris Rovers merged with their rivals Heaton Norris in 1885 and became Stockport County in 1890, following Stockport's designation as a county borough the previous year.

The town near Manchester has a name found elsewhere in the country, meaning 'marketplace at an outlying hamlet'. It is derived from Old English *stoc*, often implying a place dependent on another, and *port*, a market or town.

Motto
The Friendly Football Club.

Nicknames: *Hatters, County*
Hatters is a reference to the area's tradition of hat-making. *County* is the second part of the club name, based on the town's status as a county borough (see above).

Ground: *Edgeley Park*
Edgeley Park, named after the district, was first used for rugby in 1891. County were the first League club to share a ground with an oval ball team when they moved in with Stockport Rugby Cub in 1902, although the rugby club folded a year later. The ground may have been built on part of the Edgeley House estate, although it is more likely that it is on the site that used to be known as Poplar Grove, between Edgeley House and the Edgeley Cotton Mills.

The *Stockport Express (Main) Stand* is sponsored by the local newspaper. The *Vernon BS* (formerly *Barlow) Stand* is also known as the *Popular Side*. It is named after the local building society, which has an advertisement prominently displayed on the roof because the ground lies under the flight path to Manchester Airport. The stand had been dedicated in 1956 to the club's late chairman Ernest Barlow. The *Railway End* is so called because the main railway line from London to Manchester runs within yards of the stand. The

Cheadle (Robinson's Brewery) Stand is named after the suburb which lies to the west of Hardcastle Road. The road leads to a small public park, also called Edgeley Park, which backs on to three reservoirs, one of which abuts the ground's south-west corner. The reservoirs once served an old bleach works, which was demolished in the 1980s. The local Robinson's Brewery sponsors the stand.

Crest
The crest is basically the same as the town's, with the addition of a football, the club motto (see **Motto**, above) and the year of its foundation, 1883. Stockport's coat of arms dates back to the 1830s but has been modified over the years. It shows a blue shield, the De Stockport family crest, with a golden border and two lions. There is also a golden crown formed like a wall surmounted by a castle, presumably the Norman one levelled in 1775.

Fanzines: *The Tea Party, I O County*
The Tea Party takes its name from the Mad Hatter's tea party in Lewis Carroll's *Alice's Adventures in Wonderland* (1865, see **Luton**, Fanzine), a link to the town's tradition as the hat-making centre of the north reflected in the club nickname (see **Nicknames**, above). *I O County* is a supporters' song, containing only those words, sung to the tune of Portsmouth's 'Play Up Pompey' (see **Portsmouth**, Nicknames).

Websites: *Hatters Matters* (www.hattersmatters.com), *County Hatters* (www.freewebs.com/countyhatters/), *Hatters Mad* (www.stockportcounty-mad.co.uk)
Hatters Matters, County Hatters and *Hatters Mad* refer to the club's nickname (see **Nicknames**, above).

Stoke City

The club was formed in 1868 by a couple of Old Carthusians, old boys of Charterhouse school which had been established on the site of a Carthusian monastery of the order founded by St Bruno in 1086. The pair were apprentices at the local works of the old North Staffordshire Railway Company and with others at the works they formed Stoke Ramblers. The club dropped the name Ramblers in 1870 and merged with Stoke Victoria Athletic Club in 1878. It went bankrupt in 1908 and a new club was formed, adding City to the name in 1925.

Staffordshire's largest city has a very common name meaning 'outlying farmstead or hamlet, secondary settlement' or simply 'place', from Old English *stoc*, here implying a place that is dependant on another.

Motto
Vis Unita Portior. Unity is Strength.

Nickname: *The Potters*
The nickname is a reference to the importance of the industry that has given its name to the Stoke-on-Trent area. The Potteries, familiarly referred to as 'the Five Towns', are actually an amalgam of six towns – the major two are Stoke itself and Hanley a mile to the north, plus Tunstall and Burslem (also to the north), Longton to the southeast and the smallest, Fenton. For 400 years the district around Stoke has been Britain's main pottery and ceramics centre. The industry received further impetus when Josiah Wedgwood opened his factory at Etruria in 1769. Other famous names established by the late eighteenth century were Davenport, Minton, Spode and Copeland. Royal Doulton came from London in the nineteenth century. They all flourished because the coal needed for firing was available from the Staffordshire coalfield.

Ground: *Brittania Stadium, Stanley Matthews Way*
The club moved from the *Victoria Ground* to a new community sports stadium, named after the club's sponsors, the Brittania Building Society, for the start of the 1997–8 season. The £1 million

sponsorship deal helped to fund the cost of the 28,000 capacity stadium, built on land that had been owned by the National Coal Board and operated as Hem Heath Colliery until its closure in the early 1990s. Stoke had been at the Victoria Ground, which was named after the hotel (or Inn) opposite the Stoke End, since 1883, longer than any other British League club has remained at one ground.

The *Sentinel (East) Stand* is named after the local paper, the *John Smith's (West) Stand* is named after the brewers, the *Big AM (South) Stand* is named after the local radio station. The name of the *Boothen (North) End Stand*, taken from the district, has been transferred from the club's old Victoria Ground because this end is the nearest to the old stadium. The Boothen Terrace was where the home fans used to stand.

Stanley Matthews Way is named after the club's legendary winger known as the 'Wizard of the dribble'. Born in Hanley in 1915, the son of a boxer nicknamed the 'Fighting Barber of Hanley', Matthews made his debut for Stoke in 1932 and played his last game for the club 33 years later in 1965. He first played for England in 1934 and was 42 when he won his last cap in 1957.

Matthews was adored by the people of Stoke and when he asked for a transfer in 1938 because of differences with the management 3,000 supporters attended a public meeting to demand that he stay, and he did. However, after the Second World War he joined Blackpool in 1947. The following year Matthews was the first winner of the Football Writers Footballer of the Year award, which he won again in 1963. He was also the first European Footballer of the Year when he won that award in 1956. He was twice a losing FA Cup finalist before he lifted the famous old trophy with Blackpool in 1953 after a 4–3 win over Bolton Wanderers in a classic match that became known as the 'Matthews final' after his dazzling wing play. In 1961 he returned to Stoke and played a key role in helping the club get promoted to the First Division (now Premier League) in 1963. He retired two years later at 50 as the oldest player ever seen in the English top flight.

Matthews was awarded a CBE in 1957 and was knighted in 1965, the first active player to receive the honour. There is a statue of Matthews in Hanley, where he was born, which carries the inscription: 'His name is symbolic of the beauty of the game, his fame timeless and international, his sportsmanship and modesty universally acclaimed. A magical player of the people, for the people'. He was included in the Football League Centenary 100 players.

Crest
The crest incorporates the City of Stoke's coat of arms. The shield has an eagle in the bottom left-hand square, to show Stoke soaring above their rivals. It gives pride to the team and shows them rising above the challenges any opponent may give them. The camel in the top right-hand corner is a proud animal that shows Stoke as to be a team that commands respect and wants people to acknowledge its quality. A jar in the top left-hand corner and a scythe in the bottom right complete the coat of arms. The club's motto is included in a scroll underneath the shield. The potter sitting at the top of the crest refers to Stoke's nickname.

Fanzines: *The Oatcake, A View to a Kiln*
The Oatcake (http://stokecity.rivals.net) is named after a traditional Potteries delicacy unique to Stoke-on-Trent and North Staffordshire. A Staffordshire oatcake, which looks like a pancake, is popular with breakfast dishes such as bacon, eggs, sausage, cheese and mushrooms. *A View to a Kiln* is a play on the title of the James Bond film *A View to a Kill* and refers to the kilns used in the pottery industry.

Sunderland

A Scottish schoolmaster, James Allan of Hendon Boarding School, was behind the formation of the club in 1879 at a meeting in the Adults' School, Norfolk Street. It was originally called the Sunderland and District Teachers' Association FC. Financial difficulties meant the club soon allowed non-teachers to join. It became Sunderland AFC in October 1880.

The name of the port in north-east England literally means 'sundered land', or a 'detached estate', meaning a territory at one time separated from a main estate. The term probably had a technical sense, perhaps indicating private land set apart from common land.

Motto
Consectatio Excellentiae. Pursuit of Excellence.

Nicknames: *Black Cats*, *Mackems*
The link between Sunderland and the Black Cats goes back almost 200 years but it was only recently that it was adopted as a nickname. The team was known by a variety of nicknames, including the *Rokerites* and the *Roker Men*, until the club moved from Roker Park in 1997 and these were no longer relevant. Sunderland therefore asked the fans to choose a new nickname. The final options were the Black Cats, the Light Brigade, the Miners, the Sols and the Mackems. Almost half of the more than 11,000 people who voted on the club website chose the *Black Cats*.

The club's link with the black cat stems originally from a gun battery in 1805 on the River Wear, which was renamed the 'Black Cat' battery after the men manning the station heard a mysterious wailing black cat. In 1905 a black cat was pictured sitting on a football next to the club chairman F.W. Taylor, and three years later a black cat appeared on a team photograph. Black cats featured in several cartoons about the club in local newspapers before the First World War, and the papers reported that at the FA Cup final of 1913, which Sunderland lost 1–0 to Aston Villa, many fans wore red and white button holes with a black cat tie pin. Sunderland's match programmes of the 1930s often featured black cats on their covers. The place of the black cat in Sunderland folklore was sealed when a black kitten belonging to 12-year-old Billy Morris was believed to have brought Sunderland luck as it sat in his pocket at Wembley throughout the 1937 FA Cup Final, when they came from behind to beat Preston 3–1. For years a black cat lived at Roker Park, and was fed and watered by the club. The Sunderland Supporters' Association has used the black cat as their emblem since its formation in the 1960s. Today, the club mascots Samson and Delilah entertain supporters at the Stadium of Light.

Rival Newcastle United fans call Sunderland supporters the *Mackems*, local dialect for 'make them', a term from the shipbuilding industry which once dominated the area. Wearside ships were once sent the world over: Sunderland workers made them (Mackems) and rich businessmen (Tackems) took them away.

Ground name: *Stadium of Light*

Sunderland moved to the 49,000-capacity ground at the *Stadium of Light* at the start of the 1997–8 season, having played at *Roker Park* since 1898. The name of the new ground was kept secret until it was unveiled by the club's directors at a midnight news conference on 29 July 1997. The name was chosen, following a competition, for two reasons. Firstly, the stadium was built on the site of the former Monkwearmouth Colliery, one of the last mines to be closed in 1993, following the 1984–5 miners' strike. A famous sign at the top of the exit from the main lift in the colliery read 'Into the Light'. Sunderland wanted to maintain links to the industrial history of the site and and chose a name that would reflect the heritage of the area and honour the men who had worked in the region's collieries. The gates on the west side of the stadium have 'Into the Light' written on them and there is a miner's lamp outside one corner of the ground. Secondly, the club wanted a name that would 'illuminate' the way ahead, as symbolised by the lasers at the corners of the ground that beam into the night sky, marking out the stadium.

The name was also partly inspired by Benfica's Estadio da Luz (Stadium of Light), opened in 1954, which itself takes its name from the Lisbon suburb Luz where the Portuguese club's ground is situated. Sunderland's version was officially opened on 30 July 1997 with a friendly against Ajax.

The stands and their sponsors are the *Millennium (Fosters)*, *West*, *South (Metro FM)* and *North (Carling)*.

Crest

Sunderland's move to a new stadium in 1997 also saw the introduction of a new crest with a more complex design to celebrate the
dawning of a new era. The new badge concentrates on the mining
industry of Wearside, strongly associated with the Stadium of Light
(see **Ground**, above). This is represented on the crest by the pithead
wheel at the top of the main shield. The club motto is entwined with
the wheel. The shield is split into four sections, with two quarters
encasing the famous red and white stripes and the other two representing important symbols of the city: Penshaw Monument and the
Victorian Wearmouth Bridge. The former, a nineteenth-century
pseudo-Greek temple 100 feet long and 70 feet high, is situated just
outside Sunderland, a few miles to the west, and can be seen from
every road for miles around. It was erected in honour of John George
Lambton, the first Earl of Durham. The club put the monument on
the badge 'to acknowledge the depth of support for the team outside
the city boundaries'. The join of the bridge symbolises the two sides
of the city, north and south, which is bisected by the River Wear.
Supporting either side of the crest are a pair of lions, which also
feature on the city's coat of arms.

Fanzines: *The Wearside Roar*, *A Love Supreme*, *Sex and Chocolate*

The Wearside Roar is a reference to the noise generated by the
passionate Wearside fans. 'A Love Supreme' was the title of a Will
Downing song, in the charts when the fanzine was started. The song
has its roots in John Coltrane's seminal jazz album of the same name.
The first issue of *A Love Supreme* explained that the title of the fanzine
referred to the passion that Sunderland fans showed towards their
team.

Sex and Chocolate was launched by the editors of *A Love Supreme*.
It took its title from the slogan on an *ALS* T-shirt which read, 'There's
More To Life Than Football, But Not Much More', taken from the
Smiths' lyric, 'There's More To Life Than Books You Know, But
Not Much More'. This was combined with Sexual Chocolate, a
college band in which one of the editors played, who performed a
song of the same name. The merged title, *Sex and Chocolate Aren't
As Good As Football*, was far too long, so the fanzine was generally
known as *S and C*, or just *Sex and Chocolate*. The matchday sellers
stood outside grounds all over the country making people smile by
shouting: 'Sex and Chocolate only £1'. It lasted for thirty-seven

issues and was last sold before Sunderland's final Premier League game against Arsenal in the 2002–3 season. It was discontinued so that *A Love Supreme* could be published more often and the editors could concentrate on its website, www.a-love-supreme.com.

Website: *Ready To Go* (www.readytogo.net)
The website is named after a song by the rock band Republica. The team runs on to the pitch at the Stadium of Light to a medley of music, starting with Prokofiev's 'Dance of the Knights' from the opera *Romeo and Juliet* followed by a burst of the chorus from 'Ready To Go'.

Swansea City

The club was formed as Swansea Town at a public meeting in June 1912. It replaced 'Town' with 'City' in February 1970.

The South Wales port has a Scandinavian name meaning 'Sveinn's sea (place)' with a personal name, meaning 'boy' or 'servant' (like the English word 'swain'), followed by Old Norse *saer* or 'sea'.

Nicknames: *The Swans, The Jacks*

Swans comes from the club name. *Jacks* is from a dog called Jack who a few hundred years ago swam to sea and saved many people from drowning. The Swansea Jack pub near the Vetch Field ground is also named in his honour.

Ground: *White Rock Stadium*

Swansea moved to *White Rock Stadium*, named after the local area, from *Vetch Field* for the start of the 2005-6 season. The 20,000 capacity, £25 million stadium, built on the site of the old Morfa Athletics Stadium, was mainly funded by Swansea City Council and is shared with Swansea Rugby Club. The fans, oddly, had voted to call the stadium 'Dave'. The stands are called *Centre Stand, North Bank, East Stand* and *West Terrace*.

The site on which the club's old Vetch Field ground was situated had originally been used as a field for cultivating vetch or tare, a plant of the pea family used for cattle fodder. The ground was used by Swansea Villa during the 1880s and was first developed for sports in 1891. Swansea used it as their permanent home from September 1912.

Crest

Swansea's new badge, adopted a year after the club was taken over in 1997 by Silver Shield Windscreens, takes its lead from the City and County of Swansea local authority, which introduced a new crest in 1996 following local government reorganisation in Wales. The duck-like swan sitting above a castle, with the sea in the background, was replaced by a stylised representation of a swan. The head, neck and breast part of the crest is cleverly shaped like an 'S'.

Fanzine: *A Touch Far Vetched, Jack Plug, Jackseye, Jackanory*

A Touch Far Vetched is a play on words, incorporating the name of the club's old Vetch Field ground and suggesting that, in the tradition of football fanzines, a few stories may not be 100 per cent true. *Jack Plug* and *Jackseye* refer to the club's nickname, as does *Jackanory*, the name of a children's television programme (see **Nicknames**, above).

Website: *Jack Army* (www.jackarmy.co.uk)

The website takes its name from a terrace chant and the club's nickname (see **Nicknames**, above).

Swindon Town

Swindon Town was formed in 1881 by the Reverend William Pitt, captain of the Spartans, which was an offshoot of a cricket club. However, there is no firm evidence that he changed his club's name to Swindon Town before 1883, when Spartans merged with St Mark's Young Men's Friendly Society.

The industrial town in the north of Wiltshire has a name that means 'pig hill' or, literally, 'swine down'. The hill on which the market town Old Swindon stands was used as a pasture for swine.

Motto
Salubritas et Industria. Healthy and Industrious. The motto is also that of the town.

Nickname: *Robins*
The nickname is a reference to the team's red shirts.

Ground: *County Ground*
Swindon have played at the ground since 1895, but the club is currently looking for a site on which to build a new stadium.

The *Nationwide (South) Stand* is sponsored by the Nationwide Building Society. The Shrivenham Road cover was replaced by a stand bought from the grounds of the Aldershot Tattoo and so was dubbed the *Tattoo Stand* or the *Shrivvy*. A Tattoo is an elaboration of the evening drum or bugle signal recalling soldiers to quarters, with the music and marching staged as entertainment. The *Arkell's (North) Stand* was given its name in the late 1990s after a local brewery that has had a long association with the club. Many of the Arkells have been Swindon Town directors. In 1896 Thomas Arkell, the son of the founder of the brewery, loaned the club £300 to build their first stand at the County Ground, situated where the Arkell's Stand is now. It was nearly sold for firewood when the club hit a cash crisis in 1901 but fortunately the public rallied round and Thomas wrote off some debt so the club could continue trading. The *Stratton Bank Stand* is named after a nearby district. The *Town End* is the nearest to the town.

Crest

The current crest is the club's third, introduced for the start of the 1991–2 season to give the club a 'fresh' image after the team had been demoted from the top flight for financial irregularities, just after winning promotion. The modern design shows a red and white football speeding across a red and green diamond shape, dissected by an S for Swindon. The green section was introduced to match a new green trim on the team's home shirts. The 'travelling' football represents a club that is looking to a future of successful progress.

Fanzines: *The Magic Roundabout, The 69er*

The Magic Roundabout is a reference to the famous Swindon roundabout situated next to the County Ground and the children's television series that originated in France and has since been made into a film. *The 69er* is a reference to 1969, the year in which Swindon, then a Third Division (now League 1) team, beat top flight Arsenal 3–1 after extra time in the League Cup final.

Torquay United

The idea of establishing a Torquay club was agreed upon in 1898 by the old boys of Torquay College and Torbay College while they were sitting in Princess Gardens listening to the band. A formal meeting to found Torquay United was held at Tor Abbey Hotel in May 1899. The club changed its name to Torquay Town after an amalgamation with Ellacombe in 1910 but changed it back to United in 1921 after merging with Babbacombe FC.

Torquay is the largest and most popular of the three Devon coastal resorts that overlook Tor Bay (the others are Paignton and Brixham) and has a name that means 'Torre quay'. The quay was built in medieval times by monks from nearby Torre Abbey, which was founded in 1196. The Premonstratensian abbey (whose members were of the order of regular canons, that is belonging to a cathedral chapter) was founded at Premontre in 1119. It was situated in what are now ornamental gardens, behind the Abbey Sands beachside road. The abbey was named after the rocky hill (Old English *torr*, modern 'tor') at the foot of which it lay. The Norman church that once stood there was razed by Henry VIII, though a gatehouse, tithe barn, chapter house and tower escaped demolition. The present Abbey Mansion dates from the seventeenth and eighteenth centuries.

Nickname: *The Gulls*
The nickname is a reference to the club's seaside location.

Ground: *Plainmoor*
The club settled at *Plainmoor* in 1910.

The stands and their sponsors are the *Main Stand*, the *Carlsberg Popular Side* (the old *Cowshed*), the *Herald Express Family Stand (Ellacombe End)*, named after the local newspaper and the district, and the *Sparkworld Away Terrace*, Warbro Road (Babbacombe End). The Babbacombe End is named after the nearby district, which takes its name from the Old English Babba's *cumb* or valley.

Crest
The crest shows 'a stylised seagull' in the words of the club chairman

Mike Bateson. The gull in flight, used because of the team's nickname (see **Nickname**, above), is circled by the words 'Torquay United Football Club'. Nobody seems to know when it first appeared but the best guess is around 1988–9. The designer is unknown, though many lay claim to the honour.

Fanzine: *Bamber's Right Foot*

Bamber's Right Foot is named after the Blackpool striker Dave Bamber, who missed a penalty in the shootout at the end of the 1991 playoff final at Wembley thereby sending Torquay up into the Third Division (now League 1). At the end of normal time the score was 2–2; there were no goals in extra time so the match went to penalties. Each team scored four out of their five penalties, so the shootout went to sudden death. The Torquay goalkeeper Gareth Howells scored and Bamber, Blackpool's leading scorer that season, shot wide. Torquay were the first team to be promoted on penalties and Howells was the first keeper to score and save a penalty at Wembley. The fanzine, Torquay's first, was started after that triumphant season.

Websites: *Gulls Net* (http://torquayunited.rivals.net), *Barnstaple Gulls* (www.barnstaplegulls.co.uk)

Gulls Net and *Barnstaple Gulls* are taken from the team's nickname.

Tottenham Hotspur

The club was formed by a group of cricketers in 1882 as Hotspur FC. 'Tottenham' was added to the name three years later to avoid confusion with a team called London Hotspur. Tottenham was originally the village of a man called Totta.

The name 'Hotspur' had been chosen because of the fiery reputation of Shakespeare's Harry Hotspur, a character in his plays *Richard II* and *Henry IV Part 1*, based on a historical figure, Sir Henry Percy (1364–1403), eldest son of the Earl of Northumberland. Most of the club's founders were old boys of St John's Presbyterian School and Tottenham Grammar School, who were reading Shakespeare and were interested in this character. Harry Hotspur acquired his surname because of his frequent use of spurs when riding. The name was appropriate for the club because 'spirit' was a desirable quality for a football team and the Percy family owned large tracts of land in the Tottenham district at the time of the club's formation, hence the name of the nearby Northumberland Avenue. They were believed to have lived close to the ground in Percy House. Henry Percy is reported to have been killed in battle in Shrewsbury in 1403.

Motto
Audere est Facere. To Dare is to Do.

Nicknames: *Spurs, Lilywhites, Yids, Yiddos*
Spurs comes from Harry Hotspur. *Lilywhites* is based on the colour of the team's home shirts. *Yids* or *Yiddos* derives from 'Yiddish', the language of the club's original Jewish fans which became an offensive slang term for a Jew. It was first used in the 1980s, mainly by rival Arsenal fans, because of the large Jewish population in the Haringey/Stamford Hill area. Spurs fans turned what was an anti-Semitic chant by rival fans into a badge of honour by calling *themselves* the Yids or Yiddos.

Ground: *White Hart Lane*
The ground was originally a neglected nursery across the road from Northumberland Park, the club's first home, complete with greenhouses and sheds. Charrington's brewery, which owned the land

behind the White Hart Inn on Tottenham High Road, intended to build houses there. But the pub landlord, George Beckwith, was keen to have a football club on his doorstep because his previous establishment had been close to Millwall's ground, and he knew the profits that large crowds could bring. The Spurs directors heard of his preference and approached Charringtons, who rented them the ground, which was then named after the pub. The road was known as White Hart Lane as far back as 1600.

The stands are called simply *North Stand (Paxton Road End)*, *South Stand (Park Lane End)*, *East Stand (Shelf)* and *West Stand*. The Park Lane End takes its name from the nearby district, referred to as Park on the Ordnance Survey map of 1877. There was a hunting park in the area in the sixteenth century.

Crest

The club badge consists of a cockerel standing above a football marked with the initials THFC, flanked by a lion on each side, taken from the Northumberland family crest. The badge is related to Harry Hotspur's riding spurs, since fighting cocks were once fitted out with miniature spurs. The full club crest clearly shows these. The cockerel and ball first appeared in 1909 when former player William James Scott cast a copper statue to perch on the new West Stand. The cockerel motif has been used on the shirts since the 1921 FA Cup final when Spurs became the first and so far only amateur team to win the trophy.

The badge also includes at the top left a representation of Bruce Castle, the sixteenth-century building that now houses the local council's museum covering the history of Haringey. The museum is situated off Bruce Grove, a couple of miles from the ground. At the top right are seven trees planted at Page Green by the seven sisters of Tottenham after whom Seven Sisters Road and the Tube station are named.

Fanzines: *Cock a Doodle Doo, My Eyes Have Seen The Glory, One Flew Over Seaman's Head*

Cock a Doodle Doodle Doo takes its name from the noise made by the fighting cockerel shown on the club crest. *My Eyes Have Seen The Glory* (www.mehstg.co.uk) is named after the opening line of 'The Battle Hymn of the Republic', better known as the famous terrace song 'Glory, Glory Hallelujah', adopted by Spurs fans during the club's first, and so far only, European Cup campaign in the 1961–2 season. It became the club's anthem, especially during their successful European Cup Winners' Cup campaign of 1962–3 when they became the first British side to win a European trophy. Tottenham's late manager Bill Nicholson recalled first hearing the hymn during their European Cup campaign, as he describes in his autobiography *Glory Glory, My Life with Spurs*:

> A new sound was heard in English football in the 1961–62 season. It was the hymn 'Glory, Glory Hallelujah' being sung by 60,000 fans at White Hart Lane in our European Cup matches. I do not know how it started or who started it but it took over the ground like a religious feeling. No congregation at the biggest church assembly in the country could possibly match the noise that was to be heard off the Tottenham High Road.
>
> …The sound went all round the stadium. It was the Tottenham hymn and it frightened the opposing sides from Europe – well, most of them. The exception was the Portuguese champion team Benfica which put us out of the European Cup in the semi-final.

The original hymn was born during the American Civil War when Julia Ward Howe (1819–1910) visited a Union Army camp on the Potomac River near Washington DC. She heard the soldiers singing 'John Brown's Body', a tribute to an American abolitionist who had led an insurrection against slavery and was hanged by Colonel Robert E. Lee. Ward was attracted by the strong marching beat of the tune, and decided to replace the song's original words ('John Brown's body lies a-mouldering in the grave, but his soul goes marching on. Glory, glory hallelujah…') as she later recalled:

> I awoke in the grey of the morning, and as I lay waiting for dawn, the long lines of the desired poem began to entwine themselves in my mind, and I said to myself, 'I must get up and write these verses, lest I fall asleep and forget them!' So I sprang out of bed and in the dimness found an old stump of a pen, which I remembered using the day before. I scrawled the verses almost without looking at the paper.

The hymn appeared in the *Atlantic Monthly* in 1862. The first verse read:

> My eyes have seen the glory of the coming of the Lord;
> He is trampling out the vintage where the grapes of wrath are
>   stored;

He hath loosed the fateful lightning of His terrible swift sword;
His truth is marching on.
Glory! Glory! Hallelujah! Glory! Glory! Hallelujah!
Glory! Glory! Hallelujah! Glory! Glory! Hallelujah!

A journalist, Ralph Finn, penned his own words for the song in his book *Spurs Go Marching On* , published in 1963:

We have the finest footballers,
We've won the greatest fame;
We are supreme, we are a team,
We always play the game.
You can tell that we're the Spurs –
We'll shout aloud the name
As Spurs go marching on.
Glory, glory Tottenham Hotspur!
Glory, glory Tottenham Hotspur!
Glory, glory Tottenham Hotspur!
And the Spurs go marching on.

Glory has since become associated with the north London club whose captain Danny Blanchflower said during their great years in the early 1960s: 'The game is about glory, doing things in style.'

One Flew Over Seaman's Head refers to a goal scored from the halfway line by Tottenham's former midfielder Nayim for Real Zaragoza, which caught the Arsenal goalkeeper, David Seaman, napping in the 1995 European Cup Winners' Cup final. The goal gave Zaragoza a 2–1 victory over the holders, much to the delight of Tottenham fans who came up with the terrace chant 'Nayim from the halfway line' in honour of the much-loved Spaniard.

Website: *Glory glory net* (www.glory-glory.net)
The website takes its name from a line in the hymn 'Glory, Glory Hallelujah', sung to the tune of 'John Brown's Body', which the fans adopted as the club's anthem during their European Cup campaign of 1962 (see **Fanzines**, above).

Tranmere Rovers

The club was formed in 1884 as Belmont FC by members of two cricket clubs, and adopted the name Tranmere Rovers the following year because it sounded more important. (Tranmere is the part of Birkenhead where most of the founders lived.) 'Rovers' indicates that the club had a series of homes in their early years (see **Ground**, below).

The Merseyside district of Birkenhead has a Scandinavian name meaning 'cranes' sandbank' from Old Norse *trani*, 'crane' (a large wading bird recognisable by its long legs, neck and bill) and *melr*, 'sandbank'. Cranes must once have visited the sands that used to be visible along the Mersey river.

Motto
Ubi Fides ibi Lux et Robur. Where there is Faith, there is Light and Strength.

Nickname: *The Rovers*
The nickname is taken from the second part of the team name.

Ground: *Prenton Park*
The club played at several venues, including *Steele's Field* and *Borough Road*, which was renamed *Prenton Park* in 1895 as a result of suggestions in the letters page of the *Football Echo*. Even though it was not in Prenton, the name seemed preferable, as Prenton was a more desirable area than Tranmere. By then Prenton had lost most of its identity as a village in Birkenhead and the area derived its wealth from the nearby Cammell Laird docks and shipyards. The ground was sold to developers and in 1912 Tranmere moved to a different site just a short distance away, although they kept the Prenton Park name. In the Domesday Book the township is called 'Prestune', a variant of 'Preston'. (See **Preston North End**.) The name may also signify 'Pren's *tun*', old English for a farm or village.

The *Borough Road (John King) Stand* is named after the club's former manager, who was in charge until 1995. The *Kop Stand* is named after Spion Kop (see **Liverpool**, Ground). The name of the *Cowshed Stand* goes back to 1931 when the terrace backing on to

Prenton Road West was covered by a roof with five pitched spans, at a cost of £1,000, and was nicknamed the Cowshed. Indeed, part of the original structure came from a farm. In 1973 a gale tore through the Cowshed roof and its replacement, similar in style to its predecessor, had only three spans. In 1994 sections of the old Cowshed were sold to a farmer when a cantilevered roof with an electronic scoreboard was installed as part of the ground's redevelopment.

Crest
The quartered shield features four emblems intersected by a football, with horseshoes either side and a shepherd's staff, because the club's old ground Steele's Field was once a farmer's field. The top left-hand quarter includes the traditional English lion. The top right has a tree, representing one of the many in Birkenhead Park, one of the first parks in Britain and, almost unbelievably, the inspiration for New York's Central Park. The two smaller lions in the bottom right-hand quarter are taken from the Cheshire county crest, while the sun in the bottom left-hand quarter has its origins in the club's Latin motto 'Where there is faith, there is light and strength' (see **Motto**, above). The shield sits above the club name which appears in a scroll.

Fanzines: *White Review, Give Us an R*
White Review (http://whitereview.co.uk) is a reference to the team's white kit. *Give Us an R* is from the terrace song that spells out the club's name.

Walsall

Walsall Swifts (formed 1877) and Walsall Town (formed 1879), clubs that knew each other well since they played on adjacent pitches in the Chuckery district, merged as Walsall Town Swifts in 1888, becoming simply Walsall in 1895.

The West Midlands town has a name meaning 'nook of land or valley of a man called Walh'. 'Walh' may be either an Old English personal name or *walh*, 'Welshman'.

Nickname: *The Saddlers*
The nickname is a reference to the Black Country town's history as a centre for the manufacture of saddlery and other leather products.

Ground: *Bescot Stadium*
In 1990 Walsall moved from Fellows Park to the *Bescot Stadium*, built on the site of a former sewage works at Bescot Crescent for £4.5 million and named after the local district.

The *H.L. Fellows (Main) Stand* is named after the club's former benefactor and popular chairman Len Fellows, who was on the board from 1921 to 1938. He was also honoured in about 1930 when the club's old Hillary Street ground was named Fellows Park after him on the suggestion of the *Walsall Observer*'s correspondent Bill Rowlinson. Rowlinson, whose pen-name was 'Philistine', thought that the club should honour the man who had ensured their survival. The *Banks's Family Stand* is named after Banks's Brewery, the biggest in the area, whose full name is the Wolverhampton and Dudley Brewery. The company also owns Marston's Brewery.

The *Gilbert Alsop (Purple) Stand* is named after a former player who held the club scoring record for his forty goals in the Third Division (North) in the 1933–4 and 1934–5 seasons. Alsop also scored one of the most famous goals in the club's history during a shock FA Cup third-round victory over Arsenal at Fellows Park in January 1933. Herbert Chapman's Arsenal team, known as the £30,000 aristocrats, was full of internationals and sat at the top of the First Division (now Premier League). Walsall, whose entire team cost £69, had not won a game for a month and stood a lowly tenth in the Third Division (North). They had only been beyond the third round of the FA Cup once. Alsop headed the first goal and was brought down in the penalty area to set up the second in a 2–0 victory. The noise from the home fans could be heard two miles away. It was one of the most sensational giant-killings of all time. Newspapers checked with their correspondents to make sure they had reported the score the right way round. Arsenal fans watching a reserve match at Highbury laughed when they were told the result, thinking it was a joke. The hero, Alsop, later joined the Walsall ground staff and worked at the club for twenty years in that capacity before he died in 1992. His stand was renamed the Purple Stand when the old stand was replaced in 2003, as part of a sponsorship deal with a loan company called Purple Loans. The *William Sharp Stand* is named after a local engineering firm in nearby Bescot Crescent.

Crest
The red swift on the crest harks back to the days of Walsall Town Swifts (see above). The swift used to point downwards but the club changed the design slightly so that it pointed upwards after Walsall were promoted to the old First Division (now the Championship) in 2001. The crest also includes the symbol for leather (see **Nickname**, above).

Fanzine: *Ninety Minutes from Europe*
The fanzine's name comes from Walsall's run to the League Cup semi-finals in 1983–4, when they beat Arsenal at Highbury before losing to Liverpool over two legs, despite a 2–2 draw at Anfield. If Walsall had reached the final they would have faced Everton, who went on to qualify for the European Cup Winners' Cup by winning the FA Cup. Thus, even if Walsall had lost in the final they would have qualified for the UEFA Cup as League Cup runners-up and were therefore, retrospectively, 'Ninety Minutes from Europe' when they faced Liverpool at Fellows Park. For the record, Everton lost 1–0 to Liverpool after a replay in the 1984 League Cup final before beating Watford 2–0 in that year's FA Cup final.

**Websites: *Up the Saddlers* (http://upthesaddlers.com/wp),
The Saddlers FC (www.sportnetwork.net/mains/s44.htm)**
The websites are references to the club's nickname (see **Nickname**, above).

Watford

The club was formed as Watford Rovers in 1881. The name was changed to West Herts in 1893 and then the name Watford was adopted after rival club Watford St Mary's was absorbed in 1898.

The Hertfordshire town north of London has a name meaning 'hunter's ford' from Old English *wath*, or hunting, and *ford*, a shallow place where a river may be crossed. The ford in question was over the River Colne where hunters would have crossed.

Nickname: *The Hornets*
Watford became the *Hornets* when the club changed its home colours from blue to yellow and black in 1959, and then ran a competition to find a new nickname.

Ground: *Vicarage Road*
Watford settled at the former recreation ground in 1922. The Vicarage is St Mary's, which used to be next door to the Free School. Alan Ball's *Street and Place Names in Watford*, published by Watford Borough Council in 1973, notes 'Due to changes in the modern street pattern in the centre of the town, Vicarage Road no longer actually contains St Mary's Vicarage, but stops short at Exchange Road. During at least the first half of the nineteenth century, the western end of the (Vicarage) road was known loosely as Union Street because of the hated workhouse (now part of Shrodells Hospital) situated there.' Shrodells is now Watford General Hospital and the site of the original vicarage is now flats.

The *Rous (West) Stand* is an ambitious construction whose first stage was completed on 18 October 1986. It was built with the assistance of a £1 million contribution from the club chairman, the singer Elton John, who opened the stand. It was officially named after the club's president and the former FIFA president Sir Stanley Rous, who had died just a few months earlier.

Rous is remembered as one of the most influential figures in recent football history. He had a modest playing career but was an outstanding referee and took charge of the 1934 FA Cup final in the same year that he was appointed FA secretary. He was knighted for his services to football in 1949. In 1961 he was appointed as the sixth president of world soccer's governing body FIFA and made honorary president in 1974, a position that he held until his death at the age of 91 in 1986. Rous was the author of the simplified set of seventeen laws under which football is played today. He was a champion of properly organised coaching and active in promoting European and US competitions. He also devised the diagonal system of refereeing that is still used today. At each end of the stand are displayed the words of Sir Stanley: 'I don't want to look back instead of looking forward, but I do hope football never becomes anything more than a game.'

The *South (Rookery) Stand* is named after the Rookery silk mill that once stood next to the site and which in 1922 was occupied by the Watford Steam Laundry. The *North (Vicarage Road) Stand* was originally called the *Union Stand* and then became the *Shrodells Stand*, because immediately behind it loomed the Victorian buildings of the Union Work House, which in the 1930s were taken over as part of Shrodells Hospital, now Watford General. The corner between the Rookery and Shrodells Stand was called the 'Bend': it is there that Elton John stood as a teenager in the early 1960s.

Crest
The present crest was introduced in 1977 when the hart that is the symbol of Hertfordshire replaced Harry the Hornet, a character that in 1959 had itself replaced the black shield with red WFC on it. The club decided to use the hart because it represented the county as a whole rather than just the town. Originally, the deer sat in the diamond with a flattened top below 'W' and flanked by 'F' and 'C', each of which had one of the club's colours as its background. Now the diamond is topped by the word 'Watford'. Apart from a few minor stylistic changes the hart remains the symbol of the club.

Fanzines: *Look at the Stars, Clap Your Hands, Stamp Your Feet!, The Horn*
Look at the Stars is from the first line of Coldplay's song 'Yellow', an unofficial Watford anthem:

> Look at the stars,
> Look how they shine for you…

Clap Your Hands, Stamp Your Feet! comes from an old Family Enclosure chant sung to the tune of the chorus of 'She'll Be Coming Round the Mountain':

Clap your hands, stamp your feet, family club (CLAP, CLAP)
Hot dogs, sausage rolls, come on Watford, score some goals.

The Horn comes from the team's nickname, the Hornets.

Websites: *Blind, Stupid and Desperate* **(www.bsad.org),**
Hornets Mad **(www.watford-mad.co.uk)**
Blind, Stupid and Desperate is the title of a song by a Brighton-based
band called Earwig, and in the Watford context was an attempt at
self-deprecating humour by the website editor Ian Grant. *Hornets
Mad* takes its name from the club nickname.

West Bromwich Albion

The club was formed in 1879 as West Bromwich Strollers by employees at Salter's Spring Works (named after George Salter). The team were never certain which ground, Cooper's Hill or Dartmouth Park, they would be playing at, hence they were 'strolling' players.

'Bromwich' means a 'dwelling or farm where broom grows', broom being a yellow-flowered shrub. The club replaced 'Strollers' with 'Albion' in 1881, taking the name from the district to the west of West Bromwich town centre where some of the players lived. The district itself appears to have taken its name from a local ironworks. (See also **Brighton and Hove Albion.**)

Nicknames: *Throstles, Baggies, Albion*
Throstles (song-thrushes) recalls a caged bird belonging to the land-lady of the Plough and Harrow pub on Taylor's Lane, where the club originally had its headquarters. The birds are also native to the Hawthorn Estate (see **Ground,** below). The team adopted the thrush as its mascot and for many years such a bird was kept in a cage in the Main Stand at the Hawthorns. Superstitious fans believed that when the bird sang the team would play well. The club's emblem is a golden throstle (the Black Country word for 'thrush'), which features on the team badge. The large throstle crest that used to sit above the clock on the halftime scoreboard is now perched on a wall between the East Stand and the Birmingham Road End.

There are various theories about the origin of the nickname *The Baggies*. The club's official historian Tony Matthews lists a number of them in *The A-Z of West Bromwich Albion* (much of which is reproduced on the unofficial website www.baggies.com — see **Website,** below):

The most common theory is that it refers to the baggy shorts the players wore at the turn of the century. However, baggy shorts were worn for many years before fans started calling their team by this nickname. The nickname may come from a chant aimed at the club's turnstile operators in the early years. On match days the gatekeepers collected the takings in large cloth bags and, escorted by policemen, carried them to their office. It was not long before someone in the crowd started shouting, 'Here come the bag men!' and this developed into a chant of 'Here come the Baggies!'. 'Baggies' was also the name of the protective trousers worn by factory workers in the local ironworks, most of whom would go straight to the match after work, resulting in a very oddly attired bunch on the terraces. Joe Stringer, described as a 'walking compendium of Albion history' also suggested a link to the ironworkers, in a newspaper article in 1963:

> The name Baggies was given to Albion's ironworker fans by Villa supporters over sixty years ago. They used to put on their moleskin trousers on Saturday afternoons, with belts worn instead of braces, and periodically they would give a sailor's hitch to their unmentionables when they began to sag over their boots. When Albion and Villa clashed at the old Perry Bar Ground (pre-1897) large numbers of Albion fans walked to the game. The ironworkers kept together in groups many of them with their trousers at three quarters mast, and when near the ground, they were greeted with cries of 'Here come the Baggies of Bromwich'.

Alternatively, the nickname may have begun when supporters took bags (baggies) round to local pubs to save the club from extinction in 1905, or it may originate in the 1900s, when a number of the bigger players left and had not only their shoes but their kit filled by smaller players. Spotting their voluminous drawers, someone in the crowd shouted 'Up the Baggies'. The former club secretary, Eph Smith, suggested in *Throstle Club News* that the nickname dated from 1904 when a stocky fullback known as Amos Adams played for the club: 'His thickness of hips made his baggy pants look even more huge, and one day when he was not playing well, a fan shouted "Baggy"... the name stuck.'

Finally, the name may be a corruption of 'Magee', the name of a popular fullback in the 1920s, although this is unlikely, since Baggies was in use in the 1900s.

Albion is from the team's name.

Ground: *The Hawthorns*
The club settled at the *Hawthorns*, which sits on the border between Sandwell, in which West Bromwich lies, Smethwick and the Birmingham suburb of Handsworth, in 1900. The ground was named after the American hawthorn (Crataegus) hedges that marked the field-boundaries of the marshy area, known as the Hawthorn Estate, on which it was built. A former club secretary,

Frank Heaven, discovered a map of the farmland area and decided this would be a good name for the ground. The Hawthorns Hotel stands next to the stadium's *Birmingham Road Stand*.

The *Halfords Lane (Brew XI) West* or *Main Stand* is named after the road and the beer sold by the sponsors, the Midland brewers Mitchells and Butler (M and B). The *East (Rainbow) Stand* is also known as the *Handsworth Side*, after the nearby suburb. It takes its name from the multi-coloured seats installed when it was built in 1964. The *Smethwick End (Travel West Midlands Community) Stand* is named after the nearby district and the sponsors. The *Birmingham Road (Apollo 2000) Stand* is named after the road and the sponsors, Apollo 2000, a local gas and electrical appliances supplier, but is better known by the fans as the *Brummie Road End*.

The *Jeff Astle Memorial Gates* were erected in tribute to the club's late England striker. They stand outside the ground between the East Stand and Birmingham Road End. Born on 13 May 1942 in Eastwood, Nottinghamshire, Astle turned professional with Notts County aged 17 and as a classic centre forward was a protégé of the great Tommy Lawton. He played 361 games and scored 174 goals for Albion after joining the club for £25,000 from County in 1965. His most famous strike was the winning goal in the 1968 FA Cup final against Everton, which Albion won 1–0 after extra time. He was called up to the England squad for the 1970 World Cup in Mexico and made his debut as a substitute when England were losing 1–0 to the eventual champions Brazil but famously missed a clear chance to equalise and only managed a total of four caps.

After a number of injuries Astle left Albion in 1974 to end his career in South Africa with Hellenic. After his retirement he appeared with Frank Skinner and David Baddiel on the *Fantasy Football* television programme as a bad singer to close out the show. He died aged just 59 on 19 January 2002 of a degenerative brain disease. He had been an exceptional header of the ball and the coroner found that the repeated minor trauma had been the cause of death. A verdict of death by industrial injury was recorded.

Crest

The badge shows a throstle perched on a sprig from a hawthorn bush (see **Ground,** above) set on a blue and white striped shield. Before 1900 West Brom used a Stafford Knot as their coat of arms (see **Port Vale,** Crest), later used for big occasions such as Cup finals and European games.

Fanzine: *Grorty Dick*
Grorty Dick is a variation on Groarty Pudding, a traditional Black Country stew.

Website: *Boing* (www.baggies.com)
Boing is named after the terrace song 'Boing Boing, Baggies Baggies'. This may have originated in the terrace chant started by Woking fans who sing 'Woking Woking, boing, boing'. They either passed the song on to West Brom supporters when the teams met in a 1991 FA Cup tie or learnt it from the Baggies. Another possibility is that the chant may have originated at an away game when some Albion fans were sitting on a bench. Whenever those seated at one end jumped up and down, those at the other end were catapulted into the air. Amid the fun and games they began the chant. The song pre-dates 'boinging' (jumping up and down while raising and lowering your arms alternately), which became common towards the end of the 1992–3 season.

West Ham United

West Ham United started out as Thames Ironworks FC, a club formed in 1895 by employees of the famous shipbuilding company under the guiding force of its philanthropist owner Arnold F. Hills. When the committee wanted to introduce professional players their benefactor, Hills, disowned the club, which as a result was wound up in June 1900 and re-launched a month later as West Ham United. 'Ham' is a common name, from Old English *hamm*, which has various meanings, including 'enclosure', and 'land hemmed in by higher ground'.

Nicknames: *The Hammers, The Irons*
The nicknames reflect the team's origins as a works team in the East End docks, with the hammer symbolising the tools of a shipyard worker. The Thames Ironworks was a heavy industrial factory complex, whose main activity was shipbuilding, based at the junction of Bow Creek and the River Thames. Canning Town underground station has a wall carving depicting the Ironworks, which were situated close by.

Ground: *The Boleyn Ground, Upton Park*
The club moved to the *Boleyn Ground*, then described as a potato field or cabbage patch, in May 1904 when it merged with Boleyn Castle FC. The ground, more commonly known as *Upton Park* after the local district in which it is situated, is named after a house called the Boleyn Castle which stood next to the stadium at the end of Green Street until the 1950s. (Castle Street and the Boleyn Tavern pub also take their names from the same house.) Boleyn Castle was built in 1544, and named after Henry VIII's second wife, Anne Boleyn, though she never lived there. It was called a castle because two prominent turrets had been added soon after it was built. When United arrived both the Castle, which was being used as a school, and the adjacent field were owned by the Catholic ecclesiastical authorities. Over the centuries the house had been used as a reformatory and a priory and later became the headquarters of a bowling club. When United were promoted to the First Division (now Premier League) in 1958 a new main entrance was built on Green

Street and the last remaining turret of the dilapidated Boleyn Castle had to be demolished. The site is now occupied by the school behind the Bobby Moore Stand on Castle Street.

The *Dr Marten's (West) Stand* is named after the footwear company that sponsors the stand. An elaborate façade comprising two castle turrets, modelled on those appearing on the club crest (see **Crest**, below) has been built around the reception entrance area. The *East Stand* used to be called the Chicken Run after the primitive assembly of corrugated iron and timber used to build a cover for the East Bank. In May 1968 the Chicken Run was demolished to make way for the new *East Stand*, although the East Enclosure retains the name. The *North (Centenary) Stand* is so called because the stand, which cost £2.3 million, was opened in 1995, 100 years after the club was formed as Thames Ironworks.

The *Bobby Moore (South) Stand* is named after the club's 1966 World Cup-winning England captain. It cost £5.5 million and was opened in February 1994. Moore joined West Ham as an amateur before turning professional in June 1958. He won an FA Cup winners' medal in 1964, when he was voted Footballer of the Year, and led West Ham to a European Cup Winners' Cup triumph in 1965. He captained England to their greatest triumph, the World Cup, at Wembley in 1966 and won the Player of the Tournament award. His old adversary, Brazil's Pele, once described Moore as 'the best defender in the world'. Moore was awarded the OBE in 1967. In March 1974 he moved across London to Fulham for £25,000, having played 544 League games for West Ham. He reached another FA Cup final in 1975, ironically against his old club, which Fulham lost 2–0 and after 124 League games for the west London club he hung up his boots in 1977. Moore played 108 times for England, captaining his country on 90 occasions, and scored two goals. He went on to manage Oxford City and Southend United but failed to repeat the success he had enjoyed as a player. In the South Stand foyer at ground level stands a bronze bust of Moore, who sadly died of cancer on 24 February 1993 aged just 51.

Crest
The crest is made up of the turrets of Boleyn Castle, the house that once stood next to the ground and was named after Henry VIII's second wife Anne Boleyn (see **Ground**, above), and two crossed riveting hammers, shipyard worker's tools recalling the club's origins as the Thames Ironworks team (see **Nicknames**, above).

Fanzines: *Over Land and Sea, Ironworks Gazette*
Over Land and Sea is from the terrace song sung to the tune of 'Land of Hope and Glory':

> We all follow the West Ham
> Over land and sea (and Leicester)
> We all follow the West Ham
> On to victory...

Ironworks Gazette was named after the original *Thames Ironworks Gazette* published in the late 1800s, around the time the team was formed.

Website: *Knees Up Mother Brown* (www.kumb.com)
'Knees Up Mother Brown' was a popular song with West Ham's away supporters from the early 1960s until the late 1980s and was often heard on the road following a good win.

Wigan Athletic

Wigan Athletic was formed at a public meeting at the Queen's Hall in May 1932, following the demise of Wigan Borough, which had been formed in 1920 and was the town's fourth attempt to establish a viable football club in an area with a traditional reputation as a rugby stronghold. Borough was the first club to resign from the Football League in 1931. The new club, Wigan Athletic, was founded in the hope of carrying on in the League and with this is mind they bought Springfield Park, which had been Borough's home, for £2,850. However, they failed to gain admission to the League until forty-seven years later.

The town near Manchester probably gets its name from a shortened form of the Welsh *Tref Wigan* or 'homestead of a man called Wigan'. Attempts have been made to link the name 'Wigan' with Old English *wig*, 'war', in order to associate the town with King Arthur.

Motto
Progress with Unity.

Nickname: *The Latics*
The nickname is an abbreviation of the club's name, 'Athletic'.

Ground: *JJB Stadium*
The club moved to the £30 million *JJB Stadium* in Robin Park, a mile away from their old *Springfield Park* ground, at the start of the 1999–2000 season. The 25,000 seater stadium is named after the JJB Sports chain owned by the former Blackburn Rovers player Dave Whelan, who bought Wigan in 1995. The chain began as a single sports store in Wigan, established by J.J. Broughton in the early 1900s. The shop was bought, in turn, by J.J. Braddock and J.J. Bradburn. As the initials remained the same, the business was known locally as JJB's. When Whelan bought the store from John Bradburn in 1971, he kept the JJB name. The company now owns around 430 stores, making it the UK's largest sports retailer.

The stands are known simply as *North, South, East* and *West*.

Crest

The club uses the arms of the Metropolitan Borough of Wigan which were granted in 1974 following the Borough's formation from the merger of fourteen former districts. The black diamonds on the shield symbolise the local coal-mining industry, while the red roses represent Lancashire. The lion lying down at the top of the shield, the crowned lion to the left and the castle above are all taken from the arms of the now defunct County Borough of Wigan, granted in 1922 and used as the club's first crest. The castle represents an old castle and tower gateway to the town and appears on the town's earliest seal dating from the twelfth century. The royal lions mark Edward III's award of a royal charter to the town in 1350. The mountain ash, or Wiggin, tree above the castle was chosen as a punning reference to the name of the district. The sparrowhawk on the right of the shield is from the arms of Leigh and Atherton, two of the districts that formed the Metropolitan Borough, and originates from the arms of the Atherton family. The club's motto is included in a scroll at the bottom of the crest.

Fanzine: *Cockney Latic*

The fanzine was started in the mid-1980s by Wigan fans living and working in London who had become known as the Cockney Latic. The website is http://wiganathletic.rivals.net.

Wolverhampton Wanderers

The club was formed before the start of the 1879–80 season when a team founded in 1877 by enthusiasts at St Luke's School, Blakenhall, merged with the football section of a cricket club called Blakenhall Wanderers from the same area. Several St Luke's footballers played cricket for Wanderers.

'Wolverhampton' means 'Wulfrun's high farmstead' with the second part of the name, 'hampton', derived from Old English *hean*, from *heah*, 'high', and *tun*, 'farm'. The personal name 'Wolver', which literally means 'wolf counsel', is that of the sister of King Edgar. She was given the manor there in 985 before her brother the king endowed a church there in 994. The town also has a Walfruna Street and a Wulfran Shopping Centre.

Nickname: *Wolves*
The nickname is taken from the club name and is appropriate since Wolverhampton itself is named after a lady named 'Wulfrun', or 'wolf counsel' (see above). Supporters were calling the club Wolves long before the team's first League match against Aston Villa in 1888. The club's founder members John Baynton, John Brodie and John Addenbrooke, who started the club after being presented with a football by their headmaster Harry Barcroft, had given the team its nickname in 1877, because Wolves was easier to pronounce than Wolverhampton Wanderers.

Ground: *Molineux*
In 1889 the club moved to the *Molineux Grounds* at Whitmore Reans, which had served for twenty years or more as a central focus for sport and leisure in the town. The ground took its name from the Molineux Hotel, which was itself named after the local merchant and ironmaster Benjamin Molineux. His family was said to have 'led the fashion and tone of the town' as well as providing a major talking point by having their own black African servant. The Molineux family's origins have been traced to a seventeenth-century Willenhall family called Mullener or Mullinex. Other accounts link them to the wave of Flemish weavers who came over from Flanders with Queen Isabella in 1307, bringing with them the skills that were needed to

boost England's flagging cloth industry.

In 1750 Benjamin Molineux built himself a grand mansion, which he called Molineux House. The family lived there until 1856 after which its eight acres, stables, coach house and conservatory were sold to an O.E. McGregor in 1860. Over the next ten years, perhaps inspired by the opening of the Crystal Palace gardens and exhibition grounds in 1854, McGregor spent £7,000 restoring the house and turning the grounds into a pleasure garden, with boating lake, fountains, croquet lawns and a skating rink. He soon realised, however, that a sports ground, especially with alcohol on sale, would bring in more revenue so in 1880 he changed the name of the house to the Molineux Hotel and built a small athletics track with a grandstand around it at the north end of the grounds. The Northampton Brewery took over the grounds and in 1899 entered into negotiations with Wolves, who played their first match there in September. In those early days the Molineux Hotel also served as changing rooms. The hotel was awarded Grade Two listed status in 1977 but after being closed as a pub in 1979 it fell into disrepair.

The *Steve Bull (Molineux) Stand* was named after the club's popular former England striker, nicknamed the 'Tipton Terror', whose career had begun at Tipton Town but blossomed with Wolves in the late 1980s. Bull joined Wolves from their Midlands' rivals West Bromwich Albion in 1986 for £65,000 and played until 1999. He scored fifty-two goals in the 1987–8 season, becoming the hero of the Molineux fans. He was picked for the England squad, earning thirteen caps, scoring four goals and appearing in the 1990 World Cup finals. Bull, or 'Bully', as he is known by the Wolves faithful, is the club's top scorer with a total of 306 goals in 561 appearances, including 18 hat-tricks, and their top scorer in the League with 250 from 464 matches. A copy of his contract is contained in a time capsule set in the floor of the main foyer in the *Billy Wright Stand* (see below). He has also received an MBE for his services to football.

The *Billy Wright Stand* was named after the club's former wing-half and England captain. It was built in 1993 and officially unveiled, along with the *Jack Harris Stand* (see below), on 7 December with a friendly against Hungarian team Honved. Wolves had first played Honved in December 1954 as part of a series of high-profile televised floodlit friendlies against foreign opposition (see *Stan Cullis Stand*, below). Born William Ambrose Wright in 1924, Billy Wright joined Wolves in 1938 and turned professional in 1941 before making his international debut in 1946. He was the first player in the world to win 100 caps (for which he was made a Football Association life member) and played in all but three of England's first 108 post-war matches. He captained England 90 times including during three World Cup campaigns (1950, 1954 and 1958). One of his caps is contained in the time capsule set in the floor of the stand's main foyer. During his 541 appearances for Wolves and 105 games for England he was never cautioned or sent off. Wright was Footballer of the Year in 1952 and awarded the CBE in 1959. He made 491 League appearances for Wolves, scoring 13 goals, was a member of their Championship-winning sides of 1954, 1958 and 1959 and played a major role in their FA Cup success in 1949. One of the most popular, if not naturally gifted, British players of his era, Wright was a crowd favourite at Molineux. His marriage to Joy Beverley of the Beverley Sisters singing group was one of the most successful show business marriages: they were the Posh and Becks of their time. Wright is included in the Football League Centenary 100.

The *Jack Harris Stand* was named after the former Walsall director who was Wolves' chairman during the transitional years of 1987–92. Harris first stood on the South Bank wearing his school cap in 1938. The *Stan Cullis Stand* cost £2 million to build and was opened in 1992. It was named after the former Wolves captain and England centre half who also enjoyed an unprecedented period of success at the club as manager. Born in 1916, he made his debut for Wolves in 1934 and was a member of the side that finished League runners-up in 1938, when he won the first of twelve England caps, and 1939 when he also played in the FA Cup final, which the club lost 4–1 to Portsmouth. The outbreak of the Second World War disrupted his career. Cullis was appointed assistant manager in 1947 and the following year was given the grand title of secretary-manager. Confident, determined and renowned as a disciplinarian who was unsparing in criticising his players, Cullis adopted a highly-effective 'kick and rush' long-ball style based on pace and stamina. He claimed that the quicker and more often the ball was played into the opposing penalty area the more likely his side were to score. He assembled the most successful team Wolves have ever had, including England internationals Peter Broadbent, Ron Flowers, Jimmy Mullen, Bert Williams and Billy Wright. They won the club's third FA Cup in 1949 and first Championship in 1954, followed by another two League titles in 1958 and 1959. Had they not missed a third consecutive triumph by a point, they could have become the first club in the twentieth century to clinch the double, as they went on to win the FA Cup in 1960. Cullis left Wolves in 1964 and a year later became manager of Birmingham City, where he remained until 1970.

It was Cullis's idea to stage a series of floodlit friendlies against foreign opposition in the 1950s. After victories over Spartak Moscow (4–0) and Honved (3–2) he proclaimed Wolves as 'The Champions of the World', a claim that hastened the birth of the European Cup. Eight players from champions-elect Honved played for the Hungary team, the first to beat England on home soil, in November 1953.

Crest

The current crest features the black head of a wolf surrounded by the words 'Wolverhampton Wanderers FC', inside a motif in the shape of the wolf's head in the club's gold and black colours. The wolf was depicted leaping when it was first used as the insignia on the crest in 1968. In the 1973–4 season the badge featured three wolves, a variation on England's three lions, until they were replaced by the single wolf's head in 1979.

Fanzine: *A Load of Bull*

The fanzine's name is a play on the name of the club's former England striker, Steve Bull (see **Ground**, above).

Wrexham

The club was formed in 1872 at a meeting at the Turf Hotel by members of Wrexham Cricket Club so that they could continue playing sport at the Racecourse Ground during the winter months. Although rebuilt, the hotel still stands at one corner of the ground.

The Welsh town near Chester has an English name meaning 'Wryhtel's pasture', with the personal name (meaning 'workman', and related to the modern English suffix 'wright') followed by Old English *hamm*, 'riverside land'. There is no obvious river at Wrexham now but there was once, as demonstrated by the names of streets like Watery Road, Brook Street and Rivulet Road.

Nicknames: *Robins, Red Dragons*

Robins comes from the red colour of the team's strip. *Red Dragons* is taken from the mythical creature known as Dewi depicted on the Welsh flag, a symbol of Wales. Some say the Red Dragon (*Y Ddraig Goch*) was originally a griffin on the standard of a Roman legion headquartered in North Wales but came to be associated with the fighting dragons of Welsh legend. The significance of these dragons was proclaimed by Myrddin, the Merlin of Arthurian tales. A red dragon and a white dragon fought for many years; the white at first prevailed but in the end the red overcame the white. Myrddin prophesied that the Welsh would ultimately, after a long period of adversity, overcome the foreign invaders and maintain their language, lands and freedom. The Red Dragon became a symbol of Wales through its adoption by the Tudor ancestors of King Henry VII. Edmund and Jasper Tudor had a dragon as a crest and supporter to the arms granted them by Henry VI. When Henry Tudor faced King Richard III at the Battle of Bosworth in 1485 his three battle standards included a 'Red ffyry dragon peyntid upon white and Greene Sarcenet', which reflected his claim to be a true representative of the ancient kings of Britain and served as his tribute to the Welsh people who had made victory possible. In 1959 the red dragon on a white-over-green field, the livery colours of the Tudors, the Welsh dynasty who once sat on the English throne, was made the official Welsh flag by the Queen.

Ground: *Racecourse Ground*

In 1884 the club moved permanently to the ground, which derives its name from the horse racing staged there from 1807 to 1912. The Wrexham Races were first held under the patronage of a fifth baronet called Sir Watkin Williams Wynn, but low crowds led to their demise.

The *Sainsbury's (Yale) Stand* is named after its supermarket sponsors but still known as the *Yale Stand* after the further education college whose playing fields provide a pleasant backdrop to part of the turf that was used by the racecourse. The *Pryce Griffiths Stand* is named after the club's former chairman Pryce Griffiths. The *Kop (Town) End* is the stand nearest to the town centre and is named after Spion Kop (see **Liverpool**, Ground). The *Eric Robert's Builders Stand* is named after the local sponsors. The stand incorporates the *Marston's Paddock*, formerly the *Marston Stand* and before that the *Border Stand*, also known as the *Plas Coch goal* after the neighbouring Plas Coch, or Red Hall, area.

Crest

The club organised a newspaper competition in 1973 to design a new crest as part of their centenary celebrations. The winner was an anonymous artist whose crest shows a shield with red dragons holding a football on a red and green background. The Prince of Wales's feathers are displayed at the top of the shield by permission of the Royal Family. The Prince's motto on the accompanying scroll, the German 'Ich Dien', translates as 'I serve', and has been used by the Prince of Wales for about six centuries. The most intriguing aspect of the crest, however, relates to the dates 1873 and 1973 on either side of the scroll. Research carried out after the 'centenary' showed that the club was actually formed in 1872 and its hundredth birthday celebrations were a year too late.

Fanzine: *Dismal Jimmy*

The fanzine is named after a local journalist's description of fans unhappy at the state of affairs at the financially troubled club, which was forced into administration in 2004.

Website: *Robins Online* (http://wrexham.rivals.net)

Robins Online is a reference to the club's nickname (see **Nicknames**, above).

Wycombe Wanderers

The club was formed in 1884 at a meeting held at the Steam Engine pub by a group of young furniture-trade workers. Its original name was North Town Wanderers, thought to be called after the famous FA Cup winners, the Wanderers, who visited the town in 1877 for a match against the original High Wycombe club. The first part of the name was changed to Wycombe in 1887.

The Buckinghamshire town is 'High' as against nearby (and much smaller) West Wycombe, once a separate village but now a district of High Wycombe. However, since High Wycombe is not that high it may have the sense 'important'. 'Wycombe' comes from Old English *wicum*, a form of the noun *wic*, 'farm', required after *aet*, 'at'. The name thus means 'a place at the farm dwellings or settlement', where *wic* denotes an outlying farm rather than the main one. The present spelling has developed by association with 'combe', as in Ilfracombe, where the Old English *cumb* means 'valley'.

Nicknames: *The Chairboys, Blues*
The *Chairboys* comes from High Wycombe's tradition of furniture making. The nickname was used in the early days of the club, when many of the players worked in the furniture trade, but was only resurrected when the 1980s fanzine *Chairboys Gas* dug it out of the history books. *Blues* is a reference to the team colours of sky and navy blue, which originate from Wanderers' early affiliation with the universities of Oxford and Cambridge and their boat race teams.

Ground: *Adams Park (Causeway Stadium)*
The club moved to *Adams Park*, a new £3.5 million stadium on the Sands Industrial Estate, about two miles from the town centre, in 1990. The ground, now called the *Causeway Stadium* after a sponsorship deal, got its original name from the team's former captain, Frank Adams. He was a successful chartered surveyor, businessman and FA councillor who bought the freehold of Wycombe's previous home at *Loakes Park* in 1947 and donated it, in trust, to the club. He was patron of the Wanderers until he died in 1981 shortly after his ninetieth birthday and was succeeded by his son, also Frank (see below). Causeway Technologies, who have bought the naming

rights to the stadium, are a major provider of information technology services to the construction industry.

BCUC (Main) Stand is named after the sponsors, Buckinghamshire Chilterns University College. It is also known as the *Old Main Stand* now that the *Woodlands Stand* has been rebuilt to become the *New Main Stand*. The sponsorship resulted from Wycombe's long-term educational partnership with BCUC. The club supports the university's Sports Management and Football Studies BA Honours degree course by providing qualified FA coaching and guest lecturers. It is also working alongside BCUC on an International Football degree and a Football Foundation Course. The *Frank Adams (Woodlands) Stand* is named after the club's benefactor (see above) who followed in his father's footsteps as patron of the club and worked tirelessly to help Wycombe move to Adams Park. The stand is also known as the *Woodlands* after Sunter's Wood, which lies behind the stand to the south. The *Valley Stand* takes its name from the valley behind the stand. The *Dreams Stand* was formerly known as the *Roger Vere (Hillbottom) Stand*, but is now sponsored by a bedding company. Vere was a club director, a sponsor (through his company, Verco) and a supporter, and the extended Hillbottom Road Stand was originally named in his memory.

Crest
The light and dark blue circular crest is dominated by the Buckinghamshire county emblem of a large, chain-wearing swan, originally the badge of the Giffard and the Stafford families who once owned Buckingham Castle. The current design originated in the 1980s, with the circular version being introduced in 2001.

Fanzines: *Tales of a Chairboy, One-One, The Wanderer*
Tales of a Chairboy comes from the club's nickname (see **Nicknames**, above). *One-One* began in December 1995, taking its name from a remarkable run of one-one draws around the time of the first issue. *The Wanderer* comes from the team name.

Website: *Chairboys on the Net* (**www.chairboys.ndirect.co.uk**)
The website is a reference to the club's nickname (see **Nicknames**, above).

Yeovil Town

The club was founded as Yeovil Casuals in 1895 and changed its name to Yeovil Town FC in 1907. In 1920 it merged with Petters United to become Yeovil and Petters United, before reverting back to Yeovil Town in 1945.

The Somerset town is named after the River Yeo, earlier known as the Gifle (a Celtic river name meaning 'forked'), on which it stands.

Motto
Achieve by Unity.

Nicknames: *The Glovers*
The nickname is a reference to the town's history as a centre for glove manufacture, which was at its peak when the club was formed.

Ground: *Huish Park*
The club moved in 1920 to a ground called *Huish* which took its name from the area of Yeovil in which it was situated.'Huish' is a local term for the amount of land needed to support one family. The club moved to a new ground in 1990 but kept the old name, even though the stadium is at Houndstone in the suburbs, several miles away from Huish. 'Park' was added to the name at the time of the move.

The *Main Stand* was called the *Gerry Lock Stand*, after the chairman at the time of the move to the new ground. It was controversially renamed the *Main Stand* after the move proved to have been handled badly financially, and Lock (since deceased) was deposed. The *Copse Road Terrace* is named after the nearby road. The *Bartlett Stand* is named after the building firm that sponsors the stand. The *Westland Stand* is also named after a local company that provides sponsorship.

Crest
In heraldic terms, Yeovil does not have a crest but a shield with supporters. Its main components are the shield and one supporter (reversed) of the armorial bearings of the Borough of Yeovil. These

were designed in the 1950s from historical references. The shield contains the figure of St John the Baptist under a decorated canopy. This has been the basis of the seal of the borough for about 700 years. It represents the influence of the church on the town from the reign of the Empress Maud, who placed the Saxon freemen under the protection of the parish church of St John. On either side of the canopy is a crosier (a hooked staff or crook): one for the convent of Sion, which was granted the lordship of the borough by Henry V, and one for the Chapter of Wells Cathedral, in whose diocese Yeovil falls. Each crosier is surmounted by a gold crown, one to denote Empress Maud and one to denote King John, who granted the first market charter, thus ensuring the continued standing of the town. In St John's hand is a red circular medallion symbolising his martyrdom, with his holy lamb. The supporters are two gold lions of the Earls of Arundel. (For further details see *The Borough of Yeovil, Its History and Government Through the Ages* by John Goodchild, 1954.)

Fanzine: *On to Victory*
The fanzine takes its name from a line in the terrace song 'We all follow the...', sung to the tune of 'Land of Hope and Glory':

> We all follow the Yeovil,
> Over land and sea,
> We all follow the Yeovil on to victory,
> All together now...

The title was chosen because the first issue was released for the 2001 FA Trophy final, the first real sign that the club's fortunes were going to improve. 'We wanted to capture the feeling of the time and "On To Victory" did just that,' the editors said. Yeovil have since gained Football League status by winning the Conference in 2003 after lifting the FA Trophy in 2002. The website is www.ontovictory. co.uk.

Website: *Ciderspace* (www.ciderspace.co.uk)
Ciderspace is a play on 'cyberspace', the virtual environment of computer networks in which online communication takes place, and Somerset's famous cider.

Other books on sport from Carcanet Press